PROFILES OF THE PROPHETS:

GOD'S BIBLE MESSENGERS

Compiled by Hayes Press

Published by:

HAYES PRESS Publisher, Resources & Media,

The Barn, Flaxlands

Royal Wootton Bassett

Swindon, SN4 8DY

United Kingdom

---

1. http://www.Lockman.org

CHAPTER ONE: ELIJAH (GEORGE KENNEDY)

———

"ELIJAH WAS A MAN OF like passions with us, and he prayed with prayer that it might not rain" (James 5:17 RV Margin). However remarkable the work and privileges of Elijah, it will be profitable for us to remember we are considering a man of "like passions with us". If we keep this in mind we shall not consider him from afar but be profited through his experiences in teaching, in reproof, in correction, in instruction which is in righteousness (2 Timothy 3:16). Let us not only learn about Elijah but also learn from Elijah.

The story of Elijah's public ministry begins in 1 Kings 17, but the Holy Spirit complements the Old Testament through the pen of James - showing that his spiritual experience had a private beginning long before. "He prayed". Men of God must learn to pray privately before they may stand before kings. The man of God whom we see standing before king Ahab had first of all stood before the Lord, the God of Israel (1 Kings 17:1). There he had learnt God's Word and had prayed according to the will of God.

Elijah had prayed according to the Word of God, knowing the scripture, "You ... shall not turn aside ... to go after other gods to serve them ... The Lord will send on you cursing, confusion and rebuke ... because of the wickedness of your doings, in which you have forsaken Me ... And your heavens which are over your head shall be bronze, and the earth which is under you will be iron. The LORD will change the rain of your land to powder and dust" (Deuteronomy 28:14-24). Thus his prayer was answered with a great famine, as the Lord Jesus Himself so described it (Luke 4:25).

Concerning the background of Elijah we know very little. Rather, we are caused to consider "the Spirit and power" (Luke 1:17) which were manifested in his life. He came from Gilead, possibly from a place called Thesbon (Septuagint), a Tishbite. His tribe presumably would have been Reuben or the eastern half of Manasseh or (the writer suggests) Gad. Elijah comes to mind when we read Genesis 49:19 and Deuteronomy 33:20-21. His name means "Jah is God" and would seem to indicate that God-fearing parents had named him. It was with the truth embodied in his own name that he challenged the people on Mount Carmel. "If the LORD is God, follow Him" (1 Kings 18:21).

He was a hairy man and wore a leather girdle (2 Kings 1:8) and a mantle (1 Kings 19:19). He was undoubtedly a physically fit man who could put his face between his knees in prayer (1 Kings 18:42), could run ahead while Ahab rode a distance of some 15 to 20 miles (v.46) after the slaying that day of 850 false prophets (v.40); and on the last day of his earthly life walked perhaps in excess of forty miles from Gilgal to Bethel to Jericho to the Jordan and beyond perhaps toward the mountains of Moab.

Elijah was raised up by God with a ministry towards the ten northern tribes of Israel. King Ahab was on the throne, a wicked man with perhaps an even more wicked wife, Jezebel. "There was no one like Ahab who sold himself to do wickedness in the sight of the Lord, because Jezebel his wife stirred him up. And he behaved very abominably in following idols ..." (1 Kings 21:25-26). This woman of Zidon had brought the worship of Baal into common practice and turned the hearts of the people to her idols. Perhaps Elijah would keep the injunction that "three times in the year all your males shall appear before the LORD God" (Exodus 23:17) but we have no record of any of his dealings with Judah or Jerusalem except for one notable exception.

In character, Elijah was fearless although at times he knew what it was to be afraid. During the severe drought he had gone from the brook Cherith which is before (east of?) Jordan through to Zarephath "which belongs to Zidon". Truly a man of God under divine protection, he passed through the breadth of hostile and unbelieving Israel to the very region of Jezebel's origin. He reverenced God, covering his face in his mantle (19:13) and bowing himself down upon the earth (18:42). He was very jealous for the Lord (19:10,14) and consequently knew the loneliness, isolation, discomfort and suffering of the godly. Himself a man of decision he called for decisive action by others, saying "How long will you falter between two opinions?" (18:21). He poured contempt upon the vain hope of the people who had forsaken the knowledge of the true God (18:27). And yet the man who had stood before the king, before the people, before 850 false prophets carrying knives and lances while he taunted them, "ran for his life" before the threat of a woman (19:2-3), and gave up hope, longing to die (v.4). Possibly later also he feared when the captains and their companies of fifty men were sent to take him (2 Kings 1, noting verse 15), and he brought the fire of God down upon them.

Of interest is how this man of God appeared to others. To the widow of Zarephath and to the third captain Elijah was the "man of God". To Obadiah who feared the Lord greatly, but apparently secretly, Elijah was "my lord Elijah". To wicked Ahab he was the "troubler of Israel" and "my enemy". Well might any saint long for a similar spiritual stature through the Word of God and through prayer that it should provoke such responses from such diverse persons!

The recorded instances of Elijah's praying are to be found in James 5:17, "that it might not rain"; 1 Kings 17:20-21, "let this child's soul come into him again" ,1 Kings 18:36, "that You are God in Israel"; 1 Kings 18:42 with James 5:18, "he bowed himself down, and he prayed again"; 1 Kings 19:4, "that he might die"; 1 Kings 19:10,14 with Romans 11:2, "he pleaded with God against Israel". And there on a sad note the record of his prayer life is ended.

There are many lessons to be learnt by sinner and saint from the stories concerning Elijah but from the man himself there is a vital lesson to be learnt in 1 Kings 18,19. Elijah's great desire, expressed in prayer (18:37), was to turn the people's heart back again. And to this end he worked by fire (v.38) and by sword (v.40). But the messenger with Jezebel's threat showed that the longed-for national conversion had not occurred and he fled to Beer-sheba far south of Jerusalem, putting as much distance as possible between him and Jezebel, and cried concerning his mission that "I am not better than my fathers".

We cannot doubt his deep agony of disappointment and in consequence of it he pleaded against Israel. God fed him and then sent him to Horeb, where Moses had met God at the burning bush (Exodus 3:1) and where God had spoken to His people "out of the midst of the fire" (Deuteronomy 4:10,15). But now God will not speak in fire. First He sent a great and strong wind which split the mountain and broke the rocks in pieces, and then an earthquake, and then a fire but the Lord was not in these. He was in "a sound of gentle stillness" (19:12 RV margin). This is a lesson not easily learnt. Even the Lord's disciples asked, "Lord, wilt Thou that we bid fire to come down from heaven and consume them?", possibly having in mind the action of Elijah in regard to the companies of fifty (2 Kings 1) but the Lord turned and rebuked them (Luke 9:54-55 RV margin).

And so it was that from that time on, the Word of the Lord did not come singularly by Elijah; others were used, not by fire nor by sword but by the faithful speaking of God's Word. "Is not My word like as fire? saith the LORD; and like a hammer that breaketh the rock in pieces?" (Jeremiah 23:29). God said to Elijah, "The journey is too great for thee" and gave him Elisha for a companion and minister, while others would also speak for God. Among these were an unnamed prophet (1 Kings 20:13), and another (20:35) and Micaiah (22:8). And by the time that Elijah was to be taken up by a whirlwind there were companies of prophets in Bethel and in Jericho and in

Gilgal (2 Kings 2:3,5; 4:38) and probably even in the city of Samaria itself where Micaiah lived.

Elijah was used of God to confront Ahab in the matter of Naboth (1 Kings 21) and to rebuke Ahaziah (2 Kings 1) but over long periods (for example, three years - 1 Kings 22:1; two years - 22:51) there is no word of Elijah's public ministry. However, it may be that Elijah engaged in the teaching and preparation of these "sons of the prophets". Dear Elijah! God has not forgotten his heart's desire to turn the people's heart back again and Elijah will perhaps in a coming day labour in Jerusalem itself in preparation for the coming of the Son of Man to "turn the heart of the fathers to the children, and the heart of the children to their fathers" (Malachi 4:6). We are disposed to think that Elijah will be one of the two witnesses mentioned in Revelation 11:3-13. Their testimony will be for three and a half years during which they will shut up the heaven so that it will not rain; and in the hour of their ascension in the cloud there will be a great earthquake, causing the deaths of seven thousand. But in 1 Kings 19 God would not plead by an earthquake with His erring people.

In 2 Chronicles 21:12-15, Elijah bears his last prophetic word and it would seem that this was done by a letter prepared before the prophet's departure. Jehoram was a king of Judah, not of Israel, but he had the daughter of Ahab to wife, and the word of Elijah seems thus to have pursued the house of Ahab, to which he refers in his letter. The written word ought to have had a strong impact upon the king's mind.

Finally, we think of Elijah who had gone up by a chariot of fire and by horses of fire by a whirlwind into heaven (possibly from near Mount Nebo as we consider the places he visited on that day), coming again in glory with Moses to the mount of transfiguration, that holy mount (2 Peter 1:18) where they spoke of the more wonderful departure that Jesus was about to accomplish at Jerusalem (Luke 9:30-31).

There is very much more in the story of Elijah which could be studied with profit but we close with two points. Firstly, the twice repeated question of the Lord to His servant - "What doest thou here, Elijah?" (1 Kings 19:9,13); a searching question at any time for a servant of God. And secondly, we love the faith of the godly prophet who could hear the sound of the abundance of rain when there was as yet no cloud, not even as small as a man's hand (1 Kings 18:41,44). Elijah, a man of like passions with us, could hear by faith when sight showed nothing, and so "he prayed again".

CHAPTER TWO: ELISHA (BOB ARMSTRONG)

―――

HIS TIMES

Elisha was called to his prophetic ministry about 900 B.C. and succeeded Elijah at a time when Israel was steeped in idolatry. Truth and error existed in the same country and both were talked about in the same domestic circles. The prophet laboured in the northern kingdom of Israel, which, seventy-five years before had rebelled against the house of David under Jeroboam who was crowned king by the rebel faction in the nation (1 Kings 12). To discourage the people from going to Jerusalem to worship, he set up two golden calves, one in Bethel (south), and the other in Dan (north). These became the objects of national worship.

Evil in any dimension, whether spiritual or moral, often commences imperceptibly, and rationalizes in such terms as, "there is no harm". The playful kitten of permissiveness grows into a killer. Error is so skilful at imitating the truth. A watchful eye, and a mind taught by the Spirit of truth are very necessary. One evil made way for another in Israel, and the days of Elisha saw another system of idolatry entrenched in the nation, that of Baal-worship. An unequal yoke in the marriage of Ahab to Jezebel of Phoenicia had brought this idol into the country (1 Kings 16:29-33). King Ahab was a weak, despicable individual, unable to make a right decision: "There was none like Ahab who did sell himself to do that which was evil in the sight of the LORD, whom Jezebel his wife stirred up" (1 Kings 21:25). Baal was the male consort of Ashtoreth, the female goddess of fertility, and together they were worshipped with lewd rites and human sacrifices.

The prophets were familiar with the political and religious currents of their times. They knew and loved the law of God, and their manner of life, often involving obscurity, made them sensitive to the mind of God. Their lives were a rebuke to the godlessness around them, and their predictions of judgement were fulfilled with amazing accuracy. Their messages were black and white, and struck terror into the hearts of all who were named in their prophecies. The man of faith walks at ease with God, and in the quiet confidence that he is right because he is on God's side, and knows God is on his. Such a man was Elisha, upon whom the mantle of Elijah fell.

HIS CALL

Elisha, whose name means "God is Salvation", was the man God had ready to succeed Elijah in prophetic ministry to Israel. According to Bible chronology, Elisha's ministry lasted about seventy years, compared to Elijah's twenty years, approximately. The sovereignty of God seems the only answer to this apparent imbalance. The emotional breakdown of Elijah after the Carmel victory, and his flight from Jezebel are given by some as the reasons for his removal from the prophetic office. If God did this in every spiritual lapse of His people, not many of us would be in the service of God. His period of human weakness, an inexplicable let-down after victory such as we have all known at some time, did not take God by surprise. God did not say, "Because you have been a failure at the end of your life, you are being replaced". There is no word of censure or condemnation throughout the entire transition of prophetic office from Elijah to Elisha. There are never any emergency situations in the purposes of God: Divine sovereignty always governs what He plans. Elijah's ministry of judgement, and Elisha's ministry of blessing and healing typify the dual ministries of the promised Messiah and Prophet. One man is never a complete type of Christ.

It is evident from 2 Kings chapter 2 that there were schools of the prophets. Probably Elisha came from one of these, and was well-known to Elijah. Elisha's occupation of ploughing and sowing on the family homestead provided valuable days for preparation and meditation. He saw the value of the yoke as he turned each gleaming furrow. He knew the disciplines of sowing and harvest as part of the daily task. There is a restlessness in our generation which is affecting the disciplines so necessary to spiritual growth. Neglect of the out-of-sight roots that can only flourish through the ministry of the Spirit may be the reason that the ranks of anointed men are getting thin. Faith, prayer, reading, meditation and the pursuit of holiness are all marks of men who are taught of the Spirit. There are no short cuts or easy courses to divine anointing for the service of God. Only a renewed hunger for God and holy living can produce a revival ministry in our hearts and assemblies.

Elijah's crossing the field to meet Elisha, and casting his mantle over him was an unforgettable moment for the young prophet. His excitement to follow Elijah overlooked other higher priorities by his request that he might run and kiss his father and mother goodbye. What about the plough in the half-turned field? Should there not be some tangible evidence of renouncing the old life? Renunciation comes before consecration. Elisha understood Elijah's advice to "go back again", and on sober reflection took a yoke of his own oxen, and the ploughing instruments, tokens of his livelihood, and through fire and sacrifice provided food for the people.

These alphabet blocks of his first lesson taught him the truth of renunciation. As a priority he must be prepared, as we all must be, for a drastic shift from enjoying creature comforts to helping meet the need of others. Do not most of us have this problem in our Christian experience? The prophet's mantle was only a sign of his appointment. It was his total commitment as a bondslave of the Lord that would mark him out as God's man for the times. True discipleship is not wearing a badge, but rather carrying a cross. To be a disciple in name is one thing, but to be a disciple indeed involves following hard after Christ.

Who answers Christ's insistent call,

Must give himself, his life, his all

Without one backward look.

Who sets his hand upon the plough,

And glances back with anxious brow,

His calling hath mistook;

Christ claims him wholly for His own,

He must be Christ's, and Christ's alone.

The call of God has no options, and leaves no room for human opinion. A bondslave turns everything over to the will of another, and has no secret compartments in his life. The Lord Jesus knew this in the will of His Father. Paul knew it as a bondslave of Jesus Christ, and so on down the long line of anointed witnesses for God.

Elisha's simple act of slaying and burning for the blessing of others is an eloquent lesson of the place of self-sacrifice in the service of God. Here he must learn the truth of death to self and the world. It is at the cross we all must learn the truth that kills, before we learn the truth that makes alive, in resurrection. This was Elisha's Calvary. Dead to self and alive to God, he arose and followed. To renounce all that is sinful in our lives, and put it to death, is a requirement, the neglect of which, in our theology and practical Christian lines, lies at the root of barrenness (Colossians 3:5).

HIS COMMISSION

Before the mantle fell on Elisha, The Lord sent Elijah to Bethel, Jericho, and Jordan, no doubt scenes of his earlier prophetic labours. His request for the young prophet to wait until he returned was a test of what he had said at the plough, "I will follow thee". Three times he asked him to wait, and as many times the answer came back, "As the LORD liveth, and as thy soul liveth, I will not leave thee". The first stop at Bethel would stir many memories of Jacob's night on the stony pillow, and the vision of the house of God. How unlike the house of God the place of that early revelation had become, for Jeroboam's golden calf was there. The idol was a visual lesson for Elisha that one of his tasks was to restore the people to the worship of the true God of Israel. Jericho would recall the conquest for God of that city by Joshua. The destruction of the city which represented the idols of the Canaanites was another sign that God wanted all those nations destroyed. The visit to Jordan reminded the two prophets of the crossing by the nation more than 500 years before, and what it meant in terms of the reproach of Egypt being rolled away and the new life in the land.

Standing on the hallowed ground of these experiences would give Elisha a deep sense of the reality of his ministry as he prepared to call the nation back to God. Finally, his request for a double portion of Elijah's spirit was granted by God, for he saw his spiritual father swept up by a whirlwind into heaven. The rich endowment of the Spirit of God was like Elisha's Pentecost, and during sixty years of his ministry God worked at least eleven signs of various kinds, so that none could deny that the source of his power was the God of Israel. The areas of power were, four times over water, once over oil, twice over death, once over food, twice over disease, and once over eyesight. These are found in 2 Kings 2 through to 2 Kings 13.

Miracles in any age were never given by God to be sensational, or to satisfy man's craving for signs and wonders. Elisha's miracles were acts of divine sovereignty by which God spoke to His wayward people, to bring them back to Himself. Over Elisha's ministry could be written the words of a later prophet, "Not by might, nor by power, but by My Spirit, saith the LORD of Hosts" (Zechariah 4:6).

The fulness of the Holy Spirit is clearly taught in the New Testament for disciples of the Lord. It is not optional. It is a command of the Lord in Ephesians 5:18, and is not related to either miracles or tongues, but to praise, thanksgiving and submission to one another. The indwelling of the Spirit is historical and permanent, and His infilling is His complete control of those He indwells. It is not that we should seek more of the Holy Spirit, but that we should yield ourselves to Him. It is right that we should obey the Lord in seeking a sound Bible-based spiritual experience of the fulness of the Spirit in our lives for His glory.

ELISHA'S MESSAGE

The prophet's message to Israel was backed by one of the few brief periods in its long history when God intervened with miraculous signs. The fragmented worship of the nation no longer held any consistent pattern. Polytheism had completely broken down separation from the nations around. Except for a few godly amongst them the people were insensitive to the frightful apostasy into which they had plunged. "Thou shalt have no other gods before (literally, in front of, or above) Me" (Exodus 20:3) had long since lost its place in the hearts of an apostate nation. Children grew up to know nothing but idol worship.

Some of the choice words of Elisha that brought blessing to many are selected. To the widow of a prophet he said, "Go borrow thee vessels ... not a few". The sequel, her debt was paid. When he cast meal into the poisonous pot of stew, and assured, "Pour out... there was no harm in the pot". The beloved story of

Naaman the Syrian general, with its powerful gospel base, "Go and wash in Jordan seven times". To his fearful servant who, in the day of battle did not see the surrounding host of the Lord, "LORD, I pray Thee, open his eyes".

In profile, Elisha was a man of no compromise with evil or wicked men, sought no honour for himself, dispensed much blessing, and had this rare testimony from king Jehoshaphat of Judah, "The word of the LORD is with him" (2 Kings 3:12).

CHAPTER THREE: ISAIAH (DON McCUBBIN)

HIS LIFE

There are only the briefest details recorded about the personal life of Isaiah. He lived during the 8th century B.C. in Jerusalem (Isaiah 7:1-3; 37:2; 39:1-8). His father was Amoz, of whom nothing else is known; his wife is unnamed, but she is called a prophetess, and he had two sons who were given symbolic names. His call as a prophet took place in the year that king Uzziah died, about 740 B.C. Later he was in Jerusalem when Sennacherib's army surrounded but failed to capture the city in 700 B.C., or possibly rather later (2 Kings 19). He may well have lived on into the reign of Manasseh, from 687 B.C., and by Jewish tradition he was martyred by that evil king.

Isaiah was evidently a person of considerable standing, as he had ready access to the royal palace, and he was consulted by the kings, though his advice was not always welcomed. He wrote a history of the reign of Uzziah (2 Chronicles 26:22), and he was with Hezekiah during his illness (38:1-22). Like the other prophets he showed courage and fearlessly proclaimed an unpopular message, despite at times being mocked (28:9-10), also he demonstrated his message about the downfall of Egypt by going around for three years barefooted and in underclothes (20:1-4). He gives the impression of being a lonely man.

Besides being a great prophet, his writings show that he was an outstanding poet; this is more evident in recent translations, such as the Revised Standard Version and the New International Version, which show the arrangement of the poetic lines. His imagery and descriptions are superb, and his refrains are powerful and are seldom if ever surpassed.

HIS TIMES

Isaiah lived in a changing world, which saw the emergence of super powers with wide territorial ambitions. While Egypt had been a major power from early times, the Egyptians had shown little aggression, but now the threat was coming from the north. The precursor of these powers was Assyria, which became a major threat to other nations about 745 B.C. under Tiglath-pileser III or Pul (2 Kings 15:19). The Assyrians soon began subjugating surrounding lands, and they carried into captivity the northern kingdom of Israel between 732 and 722 B.C. The southern kingdom of Judah made an alliance with the Assyrians and became subject to them (7:17). Isaiah saw the subsequent rise of Babylon, and he even hints at succeeding world powers; it is noteworthy that during his lifetime Rome itself was founded.

All these powers would have a profound effect on his own nation, who had departed from God, and who would inevitably suffer as a result. Under Uzziah the nation had enjoyed a time of peace and material prosperity, but there was much corruption; most of the wealth was in the hands of a few, who had often obtained their possessions by fraud and violence (5:8). The wealthy women were ostentatiously displaying themselves dressed in all sorts of finery (3:16-23). The poor, on the other hand, could not obtain justice as the judges were bribed by the rich; the widows and fatherless were also oppressed.

In the shops the merchants used false measures and balances to cheat the customers. While there was an outward show of religion with the people still bringing their sacrifices to the Temple, and paying lip service to God, there was much idolatry with shrines to various gods on the hills (2 Kings 16:3-4); also spiritists and false prophets abounded (8:19). Israel's departure from God had reached the point of no return, so the people must go into captivity, though this did not take place until more than 100 years later.

HIS MESSAGE

While the book of Isaiah contains some of the best-known chapters in the Old Testament, much of his prophecy is little known. The book as a whole is not easy to understand for a number of reasons:

1. The chapters do not follow a strict historical order, but are arranged rather according to subject matter. Many attempts have been made to sub-divide the book often in hair-splitting analyses, which are anything but profitable. However, while it is fairly evident that the earlier chapters (1-39) are mainly written against an Assyrian background, it is suggested that the later chapters (40-66) are better understood against a Babylonian background.

2. The Hebrew text is obscure in parts, and this is reflected in the Authorised Version. Some modern translations are help-

ful in clarifying the prophet's meaning, but some changes are based on dubious alternative texts, for example 'sprinkle' to 'sparkle' (52:15).

3. Isaiah was lifted to the peak of prophetic vision, beyond that previously revealed to anyone else, which caused him to express things beyond his own understanding. It is evident that he did not appreciate the full import of some revelations, since although he saw in the coming Messiah 'Immanuel' and the 'Servant', there is no indication that he linked these concepts together.

4. Some of the writings express future events in the past tense, such as "He was despised and rejected of men". This is because Hebrew tenses are different from those of most other languages, in that instead of past, present and future there are only two tenses, the 'imperfect', to express incomplete actions, and the 'perfect' for completed actions. Future events therefore are normally expressed in the imperfect, but where the future is certain, as with God's prophecies, they can be expressed in the perfect, which is often referred to as the 'prophetic past'.

Over the last 100 years, radical critics have disputed the authorship of parts of the book, until eventually some attribute only about one-fifth of the entire book to Isaiah, and the rest to various later writers. The subject is too involved to discuss here in detail, and although the book has difficulties, the critics have been well answered. The authorship was accepted by several New Testament writers who directly attribute many of their quotations to Isaiah the prophet (Matthew 4:14; Luke 3:4; John 12:39; Romans 10:16,20). The unity of the book is further supported by the oldest known manuscript from the Dead Sea Scrolls, dated as the 2nd century B.C., which contain the book of Isaiah complete as we know it.

The first chapter of Isaiah is both a summary of and an introduction to the book, which starts with a striking indictment of the nation of Israel.

God calls on heaven and earth, in language similar to that used in Deuteronomy 32, to witness the ingratitude of those who have rebelled against Him, but whom He still calls His people, describing Himself as the Holy One of Israel; this is a favourite expression found frequently throughout the book but rarely used elsewhere. Although the people were observing the feasts in the Temple, their attitude made their offerings an insult to God. The following chapters (2-5) show that God still offers mercy if they will repent, but the offer is rejected as the people persist in idolatry, corruption, bribery and deceit.

It was against this background of gross sinfulness that Isaiah received his call, as described in chapter 6, when he realized his own uncleanness in contrast with God's holiness. The knowledge that he had seen God in His supreme majesty, and had yet received forgiveness of sin, was to remain with Isaiah for the rest of his life. Hence he repeatedly contrasts man's darkness with God's light, and the day of man with the day of the Lord. Thus he was sent to speak to his people who are described as deaf and blind; blind indeed, because God's light was too much for them. So the nation must go into captivity, but there follow several references to the remnant that would return to their homeland and form the nation again. The principal sin of Israel was idolatry; Isaiah speaks frequently of their rejection of God and of the foolishness of idolatry, with its confidence in man, and human wisdom.

God's concern was by no means limited to Israel, for He over-ruled all the nations, and used them for His purposes. These nations too would suffer for their wrong-doings, and the de-tails are given in a number of oracles (chapters 13-23). Whether these warnings reached the nations it is impossible to say, but the messages were as much warnings to Israel that God would punish all evil, including alliances with those nations, as these unions would not help them politically or spiritually.

Isaiah was no doubt behind the reforms carried out by Hezeki-ah, who looked for peace in his time (39:8). Afterwards the days were to become darker, but there were still the promises of a glorious future. Isaiah has been called the prophet of judge-ment, but the theme of the later part of the book is salvation.

Chapter 40 gives a message that would later bring comfort to the captives in Babylon. They appear dispirited, feeling either that God had forsaken them or that He was not the all-power-ful God, but Isaiah assures them that God still cares for them and will deliver them. "Comfort, comfort My people, says your God ... proclaim to her that her hard service has been complet-ed" (Isaiah 40:1-2 NIV). There is to be another exodus, though only a remnant would return to seek again the LORD their God. They would be delivered by Cyrus, the founder of the Persian empire, who is called the Lord's anointed (Isaiah 45:1); he would seem to be an unlikely deliverer, but God would show His power in overruling the mightiest of men.

However, Isaiah sees beyond him to God's true Servant, who would be their greater deliverer. The role of this Servant is graphically portrayed in the four Servant Songs (42:1-9; 49:1-13; 50:4-11 and 52:3 to 53:12). This Servant is going to be not only all that Israel should have been but failed to be, but also the Redeemer, who must suffer not only for their sins but for the sins of all peoples. The Songs are a subject in themselves, but they should be interpreted within their context, to show out the work of the Servant, who would combine in Himself the functions of prophet, priest and king, which none other in Israel could carry out.

The final chapters (56-66) while still looking back to warn Israel again of the cause of their suffering, describe the glory of the nation in the final victory of God. The conclusion (65-66) gives a vision of a new heaven and new earth, but still has a warning of the destiny of those who continue in rebellion.

Isaiah lived midway between Moses and Christ; he looked back to the former and on to the latter, whose life is anticipated more clearly here than anywhere else in the Old Testament. The importance of the book is amply shown by the numerous quotations in the New Testament where there are references in nearly every book, as the writers show how Jesus was the promised Messiah, and how He completely fulfilled all the prophecies concerning His Person and His work.

CHAPTER FOUR: JEREMIAH (LAURIE BURROWS)

———

THE MAN

Jeremiah was a member of a priestly family living in Anathoth, a town given to the priests of the tragic Ithamar family which was the subject of a divine curse delivered to Eli (1 Samuel 2:27-36; the connection between Eli and Ithamar can be traced from 1 Samuel 14:3, 22:10, and 1 Chronicles 24:1-6). The prophet was an outstanding member of his family, untouched by the unfaithful character of many of his forbears (e.g. Abiathar, 1 Kings 1:5-7; 2:26). He does not appear to have had any priestly duties to perform but was free to devote his whole time to his God-given work. He was divinely marked out for the prophetic office before his birth and when but a youth he received his assignment, one of the most difficult ever given to a servant of God (Jeremiah 1:5,17-19).

His natural timidity caused him to recoil from the task of speaking the word of God to an idolatrous and rebellious people but God touched his mouth and said, "Behold, I have put My words in thy mouth: see, I have this day set thee over the nations and over the kingdoms ... to break down, and to destroy and to overthrow; to build, and to plant" (1:9,10). He well knew how barren the soil was upon which he had to work and in his subsequent experience there were times when he would have refrained from utterance had not the very power of the message overcome him (Jeremiah 20:7-9).

His intense love for Jerusalem, the house of God and the people of God is clearly conveyed to us in his life and writings. God would chastise His people for their sins and Jeremiah was His mouthpiece; because of this he was misunderstood by his fellow-countrymen and lived a life of sadness and alienation from them. He lived to see the beautiful city and Solomon's magnificent temple destroyed and the divine services brought to an end. All that was left for him was to weep; weep more bitterly than he had done many years before at the death of good king Josiah (2 Chronicles 35:25). It is not surprising that he is sometimes called the weeping prophet and perhaps that is why the Lord Himself was thought by some to be Jeremiah (Matthew 16:14).

HIS TIMES

About one hundred years before Jeremiah began his prophecy, the northern kingdom of Israel was overthrow by the Assyrians. From that time, until its fall, Jerusalem underwent repeated attacks, first by the Assyrians, then by the Egyptians and finally by the Babylonians. During this disturbed period it was Judah's repeated experience that peace and safety resulted from trust in God but the lesson was never properly learnt. Even when Jeremiah came to underline God's message time and time again there was no response from a people hardened in sin.

Soon after the prophet began his public ministry Josiah, Judah's last good king, was killed in battle when he unwisely attacked the Egyptian army passing through on an expedition to the north. Josiah's successors were weak and evil men whose counsellors were unable to read the signs of the times to discern that the hand of the Lord was against them. The people were steeped in idolatry as the result of Manasseh's long, wicked reign and their return to the Lord under Josiah had been superficial (3:6-11). The mass of the people resumed their idol-worship when they were no longer influenced by the fine example of that godly king. Such was the dark background to Jeremiah's forty years' witness to an unresponsive people.

HIS MESSAGE

Apart from the occasional mention of millennial restoration, the bulk of Jeremiah's prophecies to his own countrymen are to be viewed in the light of the divine pronouncement of judgement on Judah and Jerusalem uttered during the reign of wicked king Manasseh. At that time an ingrained tendency to idolatry seemed to grip the hearts of the people and an obstinate refusal to repent manifested itself. All divine warnings were ignored until at last there was no remedy.

"Behold, I bring such evil upon Jerusalem and Judah, that whosoever heareth of it, both his ears shall tingle ... I will cast off the remnant of Mine inheritance, and deliver them into the hand of their enemies" (2 Kings 21:12-14). Such words were obviously no call to repentance and restoration, the time for this was past. It was an irrevocable pronouncement which would in some measure affect even the most faithful. Jeremiah himself was to suffer with his erring brethren. It was for this reason that, in its main trend, the prophet's message did not offer salvation to the nation for repentance, although a measure of blessing was indicated for the exercise of faith. Continuance of the divine gifts of peace and prosperity had been forfeited because the covenant condition of obedience to God's word had been broken for years without number. The long-suffering of God had at last come to an end. The same principle operates in every age. The present offer of eternal salvation by the preaching of the gospel of the grace of God to the sinner will soon end because of man's continued intransigence. May the solemn warning be taken to heart; divine judgement, although delayed, is inevitable!

One of the major themes of this prophecy was that the threatened Chaldean invasion would soon materialize. The enemy would come against Jerusalem and destroy it (Jeremiah 1:15; 25:9-11; 13:23,24; 15:1-6). Jeremiah stressed the impossibility of God changing His mind. But there was a way of escape. Those who stayed in the city and fought against the enemy would suffer starvation, pestilence, the sword and death, whereas those who surrendered, although losing their liberty, would be safe in the hands of the Chaldeans (21:4-10). But there were many false prophets who insisted that the Lord would save Jerusalem and the captives previously taken would return (28:1-4). Jeremiah firmly contradicted these falsehoods, predicting the early death of Hananiah, a prominent false prophet. This came to pass, showing to all that Jeremiah was a prophet of the Lord (see Deuteronomy 18:21,22).

An outstanding phase of the prophet's life, closely linked with his Spirit-given part in the writing of Holy Scripture, was the dictation of his prophecies to Baruch the scribe, who subsequently read to the people in the house of the Lord what was thus written. The significance of the message was not lost on the princes, who commanded Baruch to read it again to them. They realized that they had heard the word of God and knew it would anger the king whose ungodly behaviour was being so obviously condemned. So they told Baruch to go into hiding with Jeremiah while they read the book to the king. In fool-hardy defiance of the word of God the ungodly king quickly cut it with a knife and burnt it in the fire (chapter 36). His hostility towards the Scriptures of truth is strongly contrasted with the attitude of his father Josiah in similar circumstances; he was commended by the Lord on account of his tenderhearted concern that the word of God should be implicitly obeyed (2 Chronicles 34:18-28). But Jehoiakim's action could not thwart divine judgement. Jeremiah and Baruch were further commissioned by the Lord to re-write what had been destroyed, adding "many like words".

Besides prophesying to his own people, Jeremiah was given a message to the nations round about. Egypt, Moab, Ammon, Edom, Damascus, Kedar and Babylon were all included in a series of oracles which listed their misdeeds and described their imminent punishment. For some, including Israel, millennial restoration is prophesied (Jeremiah 46:25-28; 48:47; 49:6; 49:39). But for Babylon there was no such promise, she would be desolate for ever (51:59-64) as is also foretold in Revelation 18:21-24.

HISTORICAL

As might be expected the true prophet's message of doom to the Jewish people was unpalatable to them and objectionable to their rulers. Suspected of being in league with the enemy, Jeremiah was subjected to frequent persecution. Quite early in his ministry a plot was laid against him by his own family in Anathoth, but a divine warning enabled him to escape (18:18-23). On another occasion Pashhur, who was chief officer in the house of the Lord, struck the prophet and put him in the stocks for the night (20:1-6). Later, when at the command of the Lord Jeremiah stood in the court of the Lord's house proclaiming that God would make the place like Shiloh and the city a curse, he was adjudged worthy of death. He was publicly tried, but the influence of Ahikam the son of Shaphan saved him that day.

For a time Jeremiah was kept in prison in the court of the guard (Jeremiah 32:1,2; 33:1). This was in the reign of Zedekiah when the city was invested by the Chaldeans and starvation for all was looming (Jeremiah 37:21). The princes of Judah hated the prophet and obtained the weak king's consent to throw him into the lowest dungeon. There, sinking in mud, he would have been left to languish and die had it not been for the courageous and godly Ethiopian, Ebed-Melech, who persuaded the king to change his mind and order Jeremiah's rescue, which was accomplished under the Ethiopian's wise direction. Although remaining in custody in the court of the guard, Jeremiah was not allowed by the Lord to starve like the rest of the people, he was allotted a daily loaf of bread while food lasted. He was kept there in safety until the city was taken, when he was released by the Babylonian captain and well treated (40:14).

After the fall of Jerusalem the prophet was allowed to remain in the land with others whom Nebuchadnezzar chose to leave behind. However, intrigue, bloodshed and continued rebellion against the word of the Lord resulted in their going down into Egypt to escape the wrath of the now all-powerful Chaldeans. Jeremiah was forced to go with them and in Egypt he continued to remind the people of their misdeeds and consequent divine judgement. The destruction of their city seemed to have had but little effect upon their evil minds for they still persisted in burning incense to the queen of heaven in what they thought was the safety of Egypt. But Jeremiah's word from the Lord was that the Chaldeans would soon destroy Egypt and engulf them as well (chapter 44).

The prophet seems to have ended his days in obscurity in Egypt, perhaps deeply affected by the sad issue of his life's work. Few seemed to have listened or taken his message to heart. He had experienced many disappointments. He had made many enemies and few friends. All the doom he had foretold had been enacted before his eyes.

Reviewing his life, we too may wonder whether it was a failure. But it was the Lord who had said at the beginning, "I watch over My word to perform it" (1:12). With such a promise in mind we look a little deeper and consider events the prophet did not live to see. The Jewish exiles in Babylon studied his writings, particularly those which dealt with the return of a faithful remnant to Jerusalem after serving the Chaldeans for seventy years (29:10). Daniel was prominent in this exercise (Daniel 9:2), probably influencing many of his fellow Jews who, few in number but revived in spirit, undertook the long journey back to the beloved city to rebuild the house of God. So the prophet's faithfulness to the word of God had at last begun to bear fruit and God-fearing men and women have ever since found spiritual profit in the writings of Jeremiah.

CHAPTER FIVE: EZEKIEL (PETER HICKLING)

———

HIS ENVIRONMENT

Ezekiel began his prophetic work at a time of spiritual and national disaster for God's people; More than 100 years before, in the reign of Hoshea, God had "removed Israel out of His sight" (2 Kings 17:23) by permitting Shalmaneser, king of Assyria, to carry away many people from the northern kingdom, and replace them by foreigners. Despite this cautionary fact, and the continued entreaties and warnings of God, Judah had repeated Israel's sins, and in the reign of Manasseh God determined to "cast off the remnant of His inheritance, and deliver them into the hands of their enemies" (2 Kings 21:14). The execution of this sentence was delayed, but in 597 B.C. Nebuchadnezzar took Jerusalem, and carried away to Babylon Jehoiachin the king, installing a puppet king, Zedekiah, in his stead. With Jehoiachin were taken ten thousand of the leaders and the skilled men, leaving for Zedekiah only "the poorest sort of the people of the land". The king's house and the Temple were stripped of many of their treasures, and the golden vessels which Solomon made were cut up.

Among the captives was the young priest Ezekiel. He must have been grieved to see the devastation of the house of God, and must have shared in the depression of those exiles who wept by the rivers of Babylon (Psalm 137:1). The sluggish canalized rivers on the Babylonian plain would contrast sharply with the running streams among the hills of Judea; and the tremendous ziggurat, dedicated to the worship of Marduk, dominating the skyline, would be a reminder of the hostile culture with which they were surrounded. Materially, the position of the captives was not bad; they settled in communities in Babylon, where they had apparently full freedom, apart from the right to change their domicile. The skilled artisans were used by Nebuchadnezzar in building projects, and Jehoiachin and his court were given royal privileges, as the discovery of ration-tablets at the site of Babylon attests. Despite their comparatively easy circumstances, the exiles were largely in spiritual confusion, and Ezekiel was God's instrument to explain His purposes to them.

HIS CALL

After five years of captivity, the call of God came to Ezekiel, with a vision of the glory of God (Ezekiel 1). It reminded him, far from his home though he was, that his God could travel everywhere, see everything and command all things. Above all, he saw the "appearance of the likeness of the glory of the LORD". At this sight he prostrated himself, and then received his commission to speak the words of God to the children of Israel "whether they will hear, or whether they will forbear". All who would speak for God need to share in Ezekiel's experience; first, to see the glory of God, then to receive and digest words from Him. Ezekiel was forewarned that he would have a difficult task, but God impressed on him his responsibility to deliver his message; the issues both of his own life and the lives of those to whom he spoke depended on his discharge of this responsibility (Ezekiel 3:16-21). With such a hard task, discouragement would come easily, but the power of God was to harden him for it.

HIS MESSAGE

The messages recorded in the book of Ezekiel fall into three parts:

> 1) the declaration of the sin of God's people, and the imminent destruction of Jerusalem because of this sin (chapters 1 to 24),

> 2) prophecies against foreign nations (chapters 25 to 32), and

> 3) prophecies of the restoration of Israel to God's favour.

The overall purpose of the message was to assure the people of the constancy of the divine purpose. The faith of many must have been badly shaken by the captivity. They had believed that they were immutably the people of God, always entitled, whatever their spiritual condition, to His blessings by the right of inheritance. This theology had been battered by the captivity, and would be destroyed by the coming destruction of Jerusalem. Ezekiel had to point to the incompatibility of God's holiness and His people's sin, and to lead the people to repentance. Then he could show how God would once again take up His people, and establish a true worship among a just and spiritually enlightened nation.

THE DECLARATION OF JUDGEMENT

Both the method and the direction of the prophecies of judgement were remarkable. Many of them had to be acted by Ezekiel, some in conditions of extreme physical discomfort. Ezekiel 4 describes how he lay on each side with outstretched arm pointing to a picture of besieged Jerusalem, to enact the period of God's judgement on Israel and Judah. By this and other signs the prophet drew attention t9 himself as God's messenger, and when he was asked the meaning of his actions he could reply with "Thus saith the LORD ..." (e.g. Ezekiel 12:9-11). In all his prophecies he was the devoted servant of God; the characteristic phrase recurring throughout the book of Ezekiel is, "the word of the LORD came unto me, saying ..."

The prophecies of judgement were primarily directed towards Jerusalem; they described the destruction of Jerusalem, its depopulation, and the famines to be suffered by its inhabitants. However, they were apparently not delivered in Jerusalem. Why then did Ezekiel have to deliver the prophecies in such graphic detail? God had to show those in exile that the abominations done in Jerusalem justified, even demanded, His judgement upon it. Those in captivity were "a rebellious house" (Ezekiel 12:2), like those still in Jerusalem, and they had to be brought first to acknowledge the righteousness of God, and then turn to Him in repentance. It was while the prophet sat before the elders of Judah (Ezekiel 8:1) that he was taken "in visions of God to Jerusalem", where he saw the abominations which were actually taking place in the Temple. The vision showed him too the retribution of God against the offenders. When the vision had ended, he reported all he had seen to those before whom he sat (11:25) including the names of men whom they must have known, who were participating in the evil. Even these revelations seem to have brought no evident repentance; perhaps, however, they sowed the seed whose fruit was in the return of the small remnant some fifty years later.

PROPHECIES AGAINST FOREIGN NATIONS

Israel, as God's chosen people, had a special responsibility towards Him to be a holy people, but other men and nations are also judged by God according to their attitude towards Him. Ezekiel prophesied against Ammon, Moab and Seir because of their attitude towards Israel and the God of Israel; their glee at the fall of Jerusalem was to be punished by God. Tyre was self-confident in her commercial success, and her prince had claimed divine status; she was to be reduced to "a bare rock ... a place for the spreading of nets" (26:14). Egypt, too, was to be reduced so that she could no longer be the confidence of the house of Israel" (29:16). These prophecies were not all given at the same time; those against Tyre were given before the fall of Tyre, while the latest prophecy in the book (April 571 B.C.) was given after the fall of Tyre, indicating that Nebuchadnezzar would be paid for his service against Tyre by the spoils of Egypt.

THE RESTORATION OF ISRAEL

The news of the fall of Jerusalem gave Ezekiel a new credibility in the eyes of the people who could see that his prophecies had been fulfilled (Ezekiel 33:21,30). Even then, though outwardly respectful, there was little evidence of repentance in their actions. However, the Lord's message was now one of comfort and hope. Despite the failure of Israel's leaders, God Himself was to bring His sheep together, and set up His shepherd over them. In the millennial kingdom, Israel would be secure and holy. This restoration was not to be on account of any virtue in Israel herself, but to sanctify the great name of the Lord (36:23).

Judah and Israel would be reunited under one king, and would share in an everlasting covenant of peace (37:26). Dear to the heart of Ezekiel, as a priest, would be the revelation that "My tabernacle also shall be with them" (Ezekiel 37:27). He had prophesied the destruction of the old house and he knew that his prophecy had been fulfilled; now God revealed to him the details of a greater temple, in which His glory should once more dwell. Full details are given in Ezekiel 40 to 48 of the house and its environs, and it is evident that the structure is intended actually to be built. Why should there be a temple with sacrifices in the millennial age, after Christ has made "one sacrifice for sins for ever" (Hebrews 10:12)? Just as the sacrifices of the Old Covenant were prospective, those of the Millennium are retrospective, both looking to the one Sacrifice which is of any real value. In the darkest days of Israel's experience, Ezekiel was rewarded for his obedience to God by the vision of the glory of God in the midst of His people; it was a reward fitting to a man of faith.

CHAPTER SIX: DANIEL (GEORGE PRASHER)

———

GABRIEL, WHO STANDS in the presence of God, addressed Daniel as a man greatly beloved, eloquent testimony to heaven's assessment of the life of this outstanding character. Throughout the record of his life no fault is charged against him. The esteem in which he was held by his contemporaries is reflected in Ezekiel 14:14: "Though these three men, Noah, Daniel, and Job, were in it (the land of Israel), they should deliver but their own souls by their righteousness". The Lord could link Daniel with such worthies as Noah and Job as a man of notable righteousness and power with God.

Daniel is introduced in Scripture as a young man, of the seed royal or of the nobles, taken captive from Jerusalem to Babylon when Nebuchadnezzar invaded the kingdom of Jehoiakim about the year 606 B.C. He is still on record in the third year of Cyrus as receiving the great prophetic revelation of the last two chapters of his book. This was about 533 B.C., so assuming Daniel to have been seventeen years of age when taken captive, he must have been about ninety when he received this vision. Perhaps his life was then drawing towards its close, for God's final message to him is: "Go thy way till the end be: for thou shalt rest, and shalt stand in thy lot, at the end of the days". So we are able to review his character from youth to old age, a tableau of consistent fidelity to God's will. Neither the hardship and upheaval of being torn from his native land as Nebuchadnezzar's captive, nor the subtle temptations of privilege and luxury in the great Babylonian capital, disturbed his steadfast resolution to serve the Lord with all his heart.

That God strengthened His servant to maintain such high standards of dedication through a wide variety of trying circumstances is a source of great spiritual encouragement. We live in times of rapid and often revolutionary change. Ethical standards deteriorate around us. Many disciples in the more affluent countries are subject to the softening influences of material plenty. There is a development of knowledge which may cause some to fall prey to "philosophy and vain deceit after the rudiments of the world, and not after Christ". Daniel experienced convulsive political changes, involving the crushing of kingdoms and the transfer of power from one world empire to another. He was given power and affluence. He excelled in the advanced learning of his day. Yet he walked with God through it all, maintained his spiritual standards, was available to serve in successive crises, and in a ripe old age was still glorifying the God he had served so well. The Scriptures give helpful insight into the spiritual attitudes which enabled Daniel to attain such eminence from youth to old age, one keynote of his experience being that he lived consistently in the fear of the Lord.

"By the fear of the LORD men depart from evil" (Proverbs 16:6)

Young Daniel showed his true fear of the Lord in purposing not to defile himself with the king's meat (1:8). This sensitivity to observe the ceremonial requirements of the Law reveals Daniel's conscientious regard for the divine Word. It would have been easy in the circumstances to excuse himself from being unduly concerned, for he was in a strange land and under duress through the king's command. But he realized that the king's meat might include the flesh of animals prohibited by God's law to the Israelite, or the blood might not have been drawn from it, or it could have idolatrous associations. So he maintained his conscientious objection to the prescribed food, and was duly honoured by God for his loyalty to principle. This purpose to avoid defilement because of his fear of the Lord was foundational to all Daniel's achievement. It has been an example and inspiration to many, and challenges our hearts amidst all the defiling influences within and around us today. Vessels must be sanctified if they are to be meet for the Master's use.

"The reward of humility and the fear of the LORD is riches, and honour, and life" (Proverbs 22:4)

For Daniel and his three companions this word was remarkably fulfilled. They, having honoured God in the matter of the king's meat and wine, were by God honoured in their physical condition, academic progress and "every matter of wisdom and understanding". Daniel particularly had "understanding in all visions and dreams". "The secret of the LORD is with them that fear Him" (Psalm 25:14), and a crisis was soon to arise which demonstrated this to Nebuchadnezzar and all the court of Babylon. Nebuchadnezzar's exacting demand that his wise men should make known his dream and its interpretation exposed the limitations of mere human wisdom, or the resources of magic and sorcery. Daniel and his companions besought the Lord concerning the secret, and Daniel later testified to the king that there is a God in heaven who reveals secrets, the secret having been revealed to Daniel not for any wisdom that he had more than any living, but that the king might know the thoughts of his heart. Daniel's whole demeanour bespoke his humility and fear of the Lord who had revealed the secret, and to whom alone glory should be given. "Then the king made Daniel great, and gave him many great gifts, and made him to rule over the whole province of Babylon" (2:48).

"The fear of the LORD is the beginning of wisdom" (Proverbs 9:10)

There is remarkable wisdom in Daniel's approach to successive problems which confronted him. In the matter of the diet prescribed by the king, his approach to the master of the eunuchs was exemplary. He did not brusquely assert his objection or condemn Babylonian custom, but proposed a reasonable trial period of ten days on an alternative diet. This appealed to the master of the eunuchs and solved the problem for Daniel and his friends. Similar wisdom becomes the Christian disciple "ready always to give answer to every man that asketh you a reason concerning the hope that is in you, yet with meekness and fear" (1 Peter 3:15). Again when Arioch the captain of Nebuchadnezzar's guard sought out Daniel for execution (2:14), Daniel returned answer with counsel and prudence, requesting further time and assuring him that the interpretation would be forthcoming. When interpreting dreams, whether for Nebuchadnezzar or Belshazzar, there was a courtesy and humility about Daniel's approach which displayed a wisdom having its root in godly fear.

"In the fear of the LORD is strong confidence" (Proverbs 14:26)

Daniel's great moral courage has its special appeal, for he seems to personify fearless witness to righteousness in a godless society and in defiance of tyrannical power. This superb courage also derived from his fear of the Lord. With deep reverence for the one true God, Daniel could see the gods of Babylon in their puny perspective. Appreciating almighty divine power, he could look fearlessly into the face of mere human power, however terrifying, whether absolute as personified in Nebuchadnezzar, or more limited in the Medo-Persian monarchs. He courageously interpreted to Nebuchadnezzar the dream which foretold the replacement of the Babylonian by the Medo-Persian Empire. He spelt out the meaning of the dream which predicted Nebuchadnezzar's insanity, and urged the proud monarch to break off his sins by righteousness, and his iniquities by showing mercy to the poor. Before godless Belshazzar he interpreted the doom-laden message of the writing on the wall, and unhesitatingly reproved the king for his folly and sin.

After the accession of Darius the Mede, Daniel defied the death penalty, openly praying towards Jerusalem in full view of the enemies who so eagerly waited to prefer their accusation against him. The young man who had courageously refused the king's meat was now approaching ninety years of age, but he would calmly face death in the lions' den rather than compromise. From youth to maturity Daniel was motivated by a deep-seated fear of the Lord which gave him such strong confidence.

"In the fear of the LORD all the day long" (Proverbs 23:17)

Daniel's qualities as an administrator are confirmed by his holding high office under both the Babylonian and Medo-Persian administrations. Nebuchadnezzar appointed him to "rule over the whole province of Babylon, and to be chief governor over all the wise men of Babylon" (2:48). He was initially one of three presidents whom Darius set over the 120 satraps controlling the whole kingdom, but Daniel became distinguished above the presidents and satraps, because an excellent spirit was found in him, and the king thought to set him over the whole realm. Envy moved the presidents and satraps to intrigue against him; they tried to find occasion against him "as touching the kingdom", but were unable to establish any cause of complaint "forasmuch as he was faithful, neither was there any error or fault found in him". High tribute indeed! Undertaking all his responsibilities in the fear of the Lord, he maintained righteous principles in all his affairs.

To all disciples of the Lord Jesus, however lowly their calling, there is similar opportunity to glorify God through faithful service: "Obey in all things them that are your masters according to the flesh; not with eyeservice, as menpleasers, but in singleness of heart, fearing the Lord". (Colossians 3:22).

A Man of Prayer

Daniel's prayerful dependence upon God, and his deep exercise of heart for the honour of God and the blessing of His people are delightfully evident. Because he was habitually a man of prayer, he was conditioned at times of crisis to seek the needed grace and deliverance. He knew his God and therefore he did exploits. Three times a day his window was opened towards

Jerusalem as he sought in prayer towards the place of the Name the blessing which Solomon had requested long before (1 Kings 8:48).

When Nebuchadnezzar threatened the lives of the wise men of Babylon, Daniel called his three companions to seek mercies of the God of heaven. His outpouring of heart when the secret was revealed is among the choicest prayers of Scripture (2:19-23). But it is in his confession and supplication regarding the restoration of God's people and house that the inner heart longings of this great man of God are most fully revealed (9:1-19). His prayer reflects his appreciation of God's unique purpose through Israel, and the central importance of the house of God in relation to that purpose.

He set his face unto God, to seek by prayer and supplications, with fasting, sackcloth and ashes. He identified himself with an erring nation in confession of their failure. He pleaded God's merciful intervention "because Thy city and Thy people are called by Thy name". Little wonder that in response to such prayer heaven was moved, none less than the angel Gabriel being caused to fly swiftly to assure the prophet of divine response to his importunity.

"Surely the Lord GOD will do nothing, but He revealeth His secret unto His servants the prophets" (Amos 3:7)

In the practical crises which arose in his public life Daniel demonstrated the truth that the secret of the Lord is with them that fear Him. In a more specialized sense the secrets of divine purpose were so revealed to him that he was used to impart great prophetic revelations which would illumine the minds of believers through succeeding centuries. Through this man "greatly beloved", as through "the disciple whom Jesus loved" would be disclosed a vast range of prophetic truth. For Daniel's prophecies in the Old Testament and the book of the Revelation in the New Testament are complementary and constitute a major proportion of all prophetic truth yet awaiting fulfilment. Of key importance in the book of Daniel are the interpretation of the image seen by Nebuchadnezzar in his dream, and the 70 heptads (or weeks of years) recorded in chapter 9:24-27. To Daniel were particularly revealed the purposes of God through the nation of Israel, emphasis being given to those Gentile powers which would have dealings with Israel from Nebuchadnezzar to Christ and at the time of the end.

Daniel's own attitude of heart towards the revelation of divine truth invites our special interest. He was conditioned towards God to receive the light of revelation because his heart was intently yet humbly set to seek after God and the knowledge of His purposes. He have noted that Daniel and his friends had desired mercies of the God of heaven concerning the secret of Nebuchadnezzar's dream and its interpretation (2:19). He doubtless little realized that there would be revealed that night prophetic truth of such far-reaching significance. The immediate satisfaction of Nebuchadnezzar's imperious demand was of limited importance compared with the brilliant illumination of Gentile history for the instruction of succeeding generations of believers.

It would seem in keeping with Daniel's recorded attitude that he would often ponder the significance of that great image and its interpretation. He had been but a young man when the secret was imparted to him under such dramatic circumstances. Many years flowed by, years filled with responsibilities of high office, until in the first year of Belshazzar, when Daniel was about 82 years of age, he "had a dream and visions of his head upon his bed: then he wrote the dream and told the sum of the matters" (Daniel 7:1). His reaction to the dream is typical and significant: "My spirit was grieved ... I came near unto one of them that stood by, and asked him the truth concerning all this" (Daniel 7:15,16). When the interpretation had been given Daniel records, "My thoughts much troubled me, and my countenance was changed in me: but I kept the matter in my heart". Two years later (Daniel 8:1) he received the vision of the ram and the he-goat, pre-figuring the vanquishing of Persian power by Alexander the Great, and the ultimate emergence of the Antichrist from one of the divisions of Alexander's kingdom. We see again the same deep exercise of heart in Daniel: "I sought to understand it ... I was affrighted, and fell upon my face: but he said unto me, Understand, O son of man; for the vision belongeth to the time of the end". The sequel was that Daniel "was sick certain days; then I rose up and did the king's business: and I was astonished at the vision, but none understood it".

With what earnestness Daniel pursued his quest of truth as he strove to understand what God had shown him! He was among the prophets who searched what time or what manner of time the Spirit of Christ was indicating, and to Daniel it was shown that much of what he recorded was for the instruction of later generations: "Shut up the vision; for it belongeth to many days to come" (8:26). "Shut up the words, and seal the book, even to the time of the end" (12:4). "But go thou thy way till the end be: for thou shalt rest, and shalt stand in thy lot, at the end of the days" (12:13).

Daniel's earnestness in seeking to understand prophetic visions given to him by God should find an answering earnestness in ourselves upon whom the ends of the ages are come. "We have the word of prophecy made more sure; whereunto ye do well that ye take heed, as unto a lamp shining in a dark place, until the day dawn, and the day-star arise in your hearts" (2 Peter 1:19). To us also much prophetic truth may remain obscure, being more particularly relevant to those living at the time of the end. But it was the Lord Jesus Himself who rebuked God's people in the days of His flesh for their inability to understand the signs of the times (Matthew 16:2,3) and we should be concerned not to merit the same censure. Living as we do in an era of accelerating fulfilment of divine purpose towards the coming again of the Lord Jesus, we should be intensely earnest to view current history in the light of prophetic revelation. "For yet a very little while, He that cometh shall come, and shall not tarry" (Hebrews 11:37).

CHAPTER SEVEN: HOSEA (JACK FERGUSON)

WITH HOSEA WE MOVE into the group of what are generally termed the Twelve Minor Prophets, that is, the prophets with the shorter messages, known of old to the Jewish people as The Book of the Twelve. They were set in what was believed to be their historical order, a point however which is not free from doubt.

HOSEA AND HIS CONTEMPORARIES

He was the son of one, Been, his name meaning "salvation". Of his background nothing else is known, nor indeed matters. What mattered was that the word of the Lord came to him "in the days of Uzziah, Jotham, Ahaz and Hezekiah, kings of Judah, and in the days of Jeroboam the son of Joash, king of Israel". His prophetic ministry therefore may well have covered a period of some 60 or 70 years. He prophesied throughout the same period as Isaiah of the major prophets. Among the minor prophets he was for a time contemporary with Amos who spoke in the days of Uzziah, king of Judah and in the days of Jeroboam, king of Israel; and with Micah, whose messages were in the days of Jotham, Ahaz and Hezekiah, kings of Judah.

THE MAIN DIRECTION OF HIS MINISTRY

Although not stated, it is evident that Hosea belonged to the Northern Kingdom, the ten tribes known as Israel or Ephraim.

There are only eleven references to Judah in the book. His ministry was therefore directed in the main towards Israel-Ephraim, in the particularly prosperous but spiritually perilous reign of Jeroboam 2, the great grandson of Jehu, It was chiefly a ministry of strong condemnation directed against the sweeping tide of appalling apostasy in Israel. There was very little break in the clouds of judgement. In fact as one reads over the messages of all the prophets whom God sent to both Judah and Israel, one cannot fail to be impressed with the seeming endless variation in the presentation of Israel's departure from the Covenant of Sinai and the abominable idolatries and other evils to which they had sunk. In all the repetition there must surely be some profound message for us in our day; some warning of how far a spiritually privileged people can go, in falling away from the living God.

THE PERSONAL CHAPTERS (1-3)

Walking in the saintly steps of Isaiah and Jeremiah, to be followed later by Ezekiel, Hosea placed himself completely at God's disposal to be, at great personal grief on his part, an object lesson to the nation and to subsequent history. Right away in his ministry, a young man in all his purity, he was directed to marry an adulterous woman. This was neither vision nor allegory. It was simply a deeply grievous fact. This union with the adulterous woman was to be an expression of the spiritual state of the nation in relation to God. So Hosea married Gomer and she bore three children whom God named as follows:

The first boy was called Jezreel (meaning "God will sow"). It was in Jezreel that Jehu smote all that remained of the house of

Ahab, thus carrying out the desire of the Lord yet in an attitude
of complete departure of heart from the Lord. Therefore, God
decreed that the kingdom of the House of Israel would cease
(1:4). Not simply the house of Jehu: that was in any event to
cease in the fourth generation (2 Kings 10:30), and Jeroboam
2 was the third generation. But it was the kingdom of the ten
tribes which was itself to cease in due course.

The second child was a girl, called by God Lo-ruhamah (meaning "that hath not obtained mercy"), indicating that God had
decided to have no further mercy on Israel nor in any wise to
pardon her; but mercy would be reserved for Judah. The third
child was a boy, called by the Lord Lo-ammi (meaning "not My
people"), confirming that the divine intention was no longer to
regard Israel as His people. Thus in the mother, Israel's sin was
disclosed, and in the names of the children appeared the sen-
tences of judgement as a consequence.

This matter of the ten tribes having hitherto been regarded
as among the people of God raises an important issue. With
Judah, Israel still stood in the Covenant of Sinai with God.
All twelve tribes had utterly forsaken the principles of the
Covenant and the idolatrous service at Bethel was abhorrent to
God. Yet it appears that not until the apostate ten tribes were
removed into captivity did they know the revoking on God's
part of His Covenant.

Then follows in chapter 2 one of those choice developments
of generous, divine thought, tracing the course of Israel's history of unappreciative departure from her true Lover, yet fin-
ishing with the promise of another day, still future, when God

will say in infinite mercy to a believing remnant. "Thou art My people", and they will respond and say, "Thou art my God". So that the God who once "sowed" them in judgement will then "sow" them to Himself in the earth, in the great era of millennial splendour.

The final personal reference is in chapter 3. Gomer had left Hosea and the adulterous wife had gone into slavery. As an expression of the tenderness of God's love for His spiritually adulterous nation, Hosea was told to go and love and bring back Gomer. And the words of instruction he gave her form themselves into a little dispensational pearl. For just as she was to abide for Hosea for many days and not play the harlot, so "the children of Israel shall abide many days without king, without prince, and without sacrifice, and without pillar, without ephod or teraphim. Afterwards shall the children of Israel return, and seek the LORD their God and David their king; and shall come with fear unto the LORD and to His goodness in the latter days". And there the nation of Israel is today, exactly as predicted. May God speed the time of her "latter days"!

TRANSGRESSION, VISITATION AND RESTORATION - CHAPTERS 4-14

It would be very interesting to know how the messages from the Lord through Hosea reached all the people. His denunciations of the evils of the nation were well informed and devastating. He lived too close to the people not to know their ways. He lived too close to God to let them pass unheeded. The following may highlight how he laid the axe to the root of the tree:

"There is no truth, nor mercy, nor knowledge of God in the land" (4:1).

"There is nought but swearing and breaking faith, and killing and stealing, and committing adultery; they break out and blood toucheth blood" (4:2).

"My people are destroyed for lack of knowledge" (4:6).

"Whoredom and wine and new wine take away the understanding" (4:11).

"My people ask counsel at their stock, and their staff declareth unto them" (4:12).

"They sacrifice upon the tops of mountains, and burn incense upon the hills" (4:13).

"Ephraim is joined to idols; let him alone" (4:17).

"They like Adam have transgressed the covenant: ... they have dealt treacherously against Me" (6:7).

"And as troops of robbers wait for a man, so the company of priests murder in the way toward Shechem: yea, they have committed lewdness" (6:9).

In these and many other words, God through His prophet charged and warned the disobedient nation. One very dramatic warning is in chapter 5. There He says that He will be like a moth to Israel working destruction unseen among them. And like a young lion - rending, tearing and going away. And finally, "I will go and return to My place, till they acknowledge their offence, and seek My face; in their affliction they will seek Me earnestly" (5:15). And, dispensationally, Israel is there today. God has retired from them nationally. But thank God for the glorious day of 6:1 that is coming, maybe sooner than we think, the great day of Israel's national, repentant return to be raised up again into the purposes of God and live before Him in the years of Messiah's millennial splendour.

Jerome is said to have described Hosea's writing style as commaticus, that is, consisting of short clauses. That is true. They move backwards and forwards, with warnings and condemnations mingled with affectionate nostalgia, and finally rich promises of ultimate return to blessing.

In this connection the picture in chapter 11 is choice. God loved Israel as a son in Egypt. In due course His prophets beckoned forward the nation, but even as they called, so the people turned aside to worship the Baalim. And that despite all God's early care, and feeding and healing and teaching, until they became bent on backsliding and turned to other gods. But the compassions of God towards them were fathomless:

> "How shall I give thee up, Ephraim? How shall I deliver thee, Israel? How shall I make thee as Admah? How shall I set thee as Zeboim? Mine heart is turned within Me, My compassions are kindled together. I will not execute the fierceness of Mine anger ..." (Hosea 11;8,9).

This might have been a fitting climax to the prophecy, but again Hosea broke out in strong denunciation of the falsehood and deceit of Israel. Ephraim had once been powerful in her prevailing excellency among the tribes. Others trembled when she spoke. But when she allied herself to Baal and the idolatrous system of worship it was as though she died to God. Then she proceeded to add sin to sin.

Yet away deep in the heart of God He loved Israel for the fathers' sake, nor could He forget the covenant with Abraham. So the final call goes out to the prodigal nation, "O Israel, return unto the LORD thy God; for thou hast fallen by thine iniquity. Take with you words, and return unto the LORD, say unto Him, 'Take away all iniquity ...'" And looking as a seer by the Spirit's help through the centuries ahead, Hosea foresaw the day when the remnant of Israel will return in a spirit of deep response to divine entreaty, to cast off her idols forever, and be fruitful to her faithful God, throughout the thousand years of Messiah's reign - loved, healed, freely forgiven and restored.

We leave this brief meditation with a reflection on the last verse of the book, Hosea's closing comment. "Who is wise and he shall understand these things? Prudent and he shall know them?" Surely there still remain in the Word, considerable areas for study and ministry for the people of God, great fields of Israel's experiences which are rich in teaching as to the manner of the God whose we are and whom we seek to serve.

CHAPTER EIGHT: AMOS (MARTIN ARCHIBALD)

———

THE BOOK OF AMOS HAS an important place in 'The Book of the Twelve Prophets', as the first in composition and as an outstanding example of literary skill. Yet the author is introduced in chapter 1 not as a professional prophet or writer, but as a herdsman or sheep-farmer, the man who marked the sheep, and so was either a responsible tender or the owner. In chapter 7 he is described as cattle-tender and sycamore-grower. The absence of the usual word for shepherd, the 'pasturer' of Isaiah 40:11, and Amos's freedom to travel from Judah to Israel suggest a man of some means, albeit hard-won. This is consistent with the sideline of tending sycamores, which produced a poor type of fruit, but because of the altitude of Tekoa would have to be grown in fields leased in the land sloping eastwards to the Jordan valley. He refuses in Amos 7:14 to be classed as a member of the many Hebrew schools of prophets who might earn their bread by fees, and who often attacked the government. This is a defence of the integrity and authority of his message (7:15), for he refers with respect (2:11, 3:7) to the prophets that clearly spoke from God.

Like David, alone on the hills caring for his sheep, he has plainly learned watchfulness and dependence on God. But living within eleven miles of Jerusalem, and looking down towards, and perhaps dealing with, traders on the caravan-route to Egypt and Arabia, his knowledge of men and affairs is greater than we would expect of a writer from a small community. He is acquainted with the origins and characters of peoples from Tyre to Edom, from Ethiopia to Kir (in Babylonia), the geography of Israel, and the behaviour of the Nile. This the Spirit turns to account in speaking with authority to the Northern kingdom. In addition, we can feel Amos's power as a writer in the vivid imagery in chapter 3; or the memorable pictures of the brand plucked out of the burning, God turning the shadow of death into morning, horses running on the rock, the ploughman overtaking the reaper. Samaria's rulers are reproached with stinging double meaning at 6:1: "the notable men of the chief of the nations".

The prophet also had courage. Though coming from another country, and only a private citizen, he fearlessly replies to the king's priest at Bethel that his wife will become a harlot, and his family will not even go forth as prisoners of war, but will be killed. Some then say Amos lacks warmth, but consider how deeply he cares about the atrocities of Ammon and Moab (1:13,2:1), and the plight of the poor and oppressed, and how he pleads, Moses-like, for Israel before the Lord (7:2,5). We may ask why Amos was sent to another kingdom. It is a lesson to us in God's freedom to use whom He chooses. When no vessel could be found in Israel, one fit for His purpose could be brought from the poorer Southern nation, most unexpectedly to men, while Hosea, who writes from the point of view of a citizen of Israel (Hosea 7:1-5), was used later to deal particularly with Israel's idolatry.

Amos was the first of the writing prophets. The oral prophets succeeded in leading the people and influencing events; henceforth the messenger's warning was to be set down in record against those who would no longer hear. Yet Zechariah and Haggai, whose ministry is recorded, had an immediate effect on their hearers (Ezra 5:1,2), and we may suppose some heeded Amos. An Ethiopian eunuch trusted in God when Jeremiah spoke to the final generation of the kingdom of Judah. To Amos's record we also owe some history that does not appear in the chroniclers' books - for example, the hardship described in 4:6-8.

CREATION OF WEALTH IN THE AFFLUENT SOCIETY

During the period of overlap in the rules of Jeroboam II of Israel and Uzziah of Judah, which would be the last fourteen years of Jeroboam's reign - long enough for Amos's ministry to Israel to begin and end the Northern kingdom must have been very conscious of the relief caused by God's overrule among their enemies. For the second half of the previous century they had lived under harassment by Syria, and two reigns before had even been overrun, together with Judah. One reign before Amos's prophecy, however, Syria was weakened by the attacks of the Assyrians and the king of Hamath, Joash defeated Benhadad III on three occasions, and Jeroboam II "recovered Damascus", so that Israel could on three fronts claim again the boundaries of Solomon (1 Kings 8:65) and Moses' commandment (Numbers 34:8,11). Then, in a striking example of God's disposition of the peoples to benefit His own, Assyria's trouble with Urartu to the east and conspiracy at home prevented her from reaching beyond Syria westwards. Now the class that organized profits from the new security and increase in trade built their own houses in dressed stone, with separate summer and winter quarters, using craftsmen who had learned from the period of close relations with Tyre and Sidon. In rooms with couches fitted round three walls below ivory relief work, the corner-seat opposite the door being the most sumptuous (see 3:12), the rich became accustomed to selected lamb and stall-reared calf, and served their wine in festival bowls. These comforts had become more important to them than the God they professed to serve, as can happen today; while the poor increased in numbers and were exploited and oppressed.

THE ORACLES (CHAPTERS 1 AND 2)

This pursuit of material things Amos attacks with a series of poems that can be read in three groups oracles (or brief prophecies of punishment), sermons, and visions. These he heads with a text (1:2) reminding the ten tribes about Zion, God's centre, from which they should have learned faithfulness in worship. Moreover, the prophecy will be as certain as the word of God has always proved to be, for even the lofty ridge of Carmel, so fertile that its name means 'garden-land', will be blasted when the thunder of judgement comes. After this vigorous opening, so offensive to Northern ears, Amos turns to the people surrounding Israel and Judah, who were to receive judgement over the same period of time as they, because the power God was using was to overrun the whole of Palestine, even to Egypt. Secular history attributes the prosperity or decline of these peoples to changes in the strength of the dominant power, Assyria, until her fall before Babylon. But in the divine writings, the Holy Spirit traces the spiritual lessons of those days in the ways of God.

The nations in Amos 1 had each seen in Israel in her finest days the witness to God's goodness. They had been tested in their relations with a people instructed in God's holiness and power to bless. Now they had shown their unchanged characters; and people who have known the grace of God merit greater judgement. Thus Amos uses the word 'transgressions' for their sins, since they are offences against instruction or commandment. Hence also the forcefulness of the word when used in Amos 4:4 of Israel's pilgrimages to Bethel and Gilgal for sacrifice.

AN ADVERSARY ROUND ABOUT THE LAND (3:1-4:3)

As though the oracles were intended to shock the people into attention, Amos adjures them, "Hear this word ...", the repeated introduction to the 'sermons'. They were confident that after success against Syria, they had security for the foreseeable future, with strong neighbours to the east, and Judah and Edom dealt with (2 Kings 14:7-14). But it was exactly this defence that would be swept away first, Amos was saying; the oppressors would overrun the neighbouring lands on their way to Israel, who had now become like one of them. It has been remarked that Amos does not mention the nation that would be used to judge Israel.

Similarly Hosea, writing later in the century (cp. Amos 1:1 and Hosea 1:1) and thus nearer to the event, only warns them of the folly of a covenant with Assyria. So the prophet's task is to state that vengeance, ordained of God, assuredly will come, and concentrate on showing Israel their present error. To say that the agent would be a nation as remote and unknown as

Assyria would not have made the prophecy any more credible. The graphic description of the conquerors' methods would be enough to convince them that the prophet had been shown a real event (e.g. 6:10).

"SEEK YE ME AND YE SHALL LIVE" (4:4-5:17)

From Dan to Bethel there was an impressive amount of religious activity. Thus occupied, Israel did not recognize the warning of recent disasters to crops. But Amos was to open the worshippers' eyes to their true condition. Selfishness in their lives went with perversion in worship. They would even go 45 miles south of Jerusalem to reach Beersheba, revered because of its association with Isaac, and so their offerings were polluted with transgression (4:4). The Lord that "treadeth upon the high places of the earth" (4:13) needed no such eminences as the high places of Isaac (7:9), and to obey Him is better than sacrifice.

The people's principal evil has been to place their own desires before the claims of God; they are diseased with covetousness. The display of sacrifice and festival is financed by what the rich have extorted from the poor. They have forced up prices for their crops, absorbed the smallholdings into large estates, and thwarted the administration of justice in the gate (of the cities, where judges sat), so that those dispossessed of their inheritance cannot obtain redress (5:12). But covetousness is idolatry (Colossians 3:5), and with such conduct they cannot claim to know the goodness of God. The only cure is to seek the Lord, the One who alone is good, in faithfulness - not the places of false worship, and a mere form of godliness whose power is denied. Otherwise, they will become a prey to evil in the very areas of their inheritance that they have abused. "Blessed are the pure in heart" said the Lord: "for they shall see God".

RIGHTEOUSNESS AS AN EVERFLOWING STREAM (5:1-6:14)

The word of the Lord becomes two expressions of woe to those who cannot recognize His character (5:18, 6:1). Amos supremely teaches Israel what they had been told through Moses at the beginning, that the Lord Jehovah is the God of justice and mercy, safeguarding the poor and the exploited of whatever degree (Leviticus 25:35 etc., but see also 19:15). Like men of our own time, Israel and Judah sought earthly things before the kingdom of God and His righteousness. The uprightness of those blessed by God ought to be steady and consistent, not like the Palestine river that was a torrent in winter, and a trickle or dry bed when the herdman came to it with his flock in summer (5:24 RVM). Israel's tribute of sacrifice was corrupt, echoing the wickedness of their homes; and here judgement would fall, when a relative called to a refugee hiding in the innermost parts of a pillaged house, "Is there any with thee?" and hushed his reply, "for we may not mention the name of the LORD" for very despair.

THE VISIONS (7-9:10)

Two judgements the prophet successfully pleads against. The first comes in the farmer's language of the latter growth after the king's mowings. The second crop, that the common people needed for their cattle or themselves, was to be destroyed. The second punishment, of fire, is as drastic as the flood which God has promised will not come again. The third vision would appeal to craftsmen - the plumb-line that will be God's standard in testing the rectitude of their conduct (cp. Isaiah. 28:17). The picture would be the more frightening because walls could be destroyed with such thoroughness as if a plumb-line were being used (Lamentations 2:8). Again comes a vision for people to whom harvest-time was very important - the picture of Israel as a basket of summer fruit - the last of the crop, late and poor; Amos the poet reminds them how the Hebrew word for "summer" is so like that for the "end". In the fifth vision, the Lord Himself declares that those who flee shall not escape - though they should hide themselves 1,800 feet high on Carmel, in the famous labyrinths of limestone caves (9:3).

THE WORD OF PROPHECY MADE MORE SURE

Chapter 9:11-15 describes the true prosperity from God, which makes rich and adds no sorrow, picking up again the weaknesses Amos had pointed out in Israel's present ease. The barren places, not just the fertile plains, will be the source of corn and wine; the cities they build will have inhabitants; and from what they plant, they will be sure of reaping. In verses 11 and 12 he thinks of the king taken from following the flock to lead a nation. David's house of cedar led him to make provision for a temple that would be exceeding magnifical; but in Acts 15:16-18 James, as New Testament prophet, opens this vision and its present realization to people of all the countries this magazine reaches. Today disciples of Christ can come to the place of the Name and there be builded together to serve God, in the beauty of holiness that belongs to His pattern.

CHAPTER NINE: JONAH (KEN RILEY)

———

THE BOOK OF JONAH HAS probably been attacked and ridiculed more than any other part of the Scriptures. Even Josephus wrote in apologetic tones of the book and would not commit himself to believing the story when he recorded Jewish history for his Roman masters. For those who wanted to keep it in the Scriptures but not acknowledge its veracity, the book has been treated as an allegory and many and varied have been the interpretations placed upon it, the most common being that Israel should cease to be inward-looking and realize more its evangelistic responsibilities towards its neighbours.

The born-again believer, however, will accept completely the veracity of the book because the Lord Jesus gave it His seal when He said, "For as Jonah was three days and three nights in the belly of the sea-monster; so shall the Son of man be three days and three nights in the heart of the earth" (Matthew 12:40 RV margin). Thus from the lips of the One who could say, "I am ... the truth" we have all the confirmation we need that the book should command our close attention.

Jonah came from Gath-hepher, a village between Nazareth and Cana. He was thus of the tribe of Zebulun and a native of Galilee. Re lived during the days of Jeroboam II (c. 793-753 B.C.) and was used of God to tell that king of the expansion of Israel's borders (2 Kings 14:25). With Assyria pre-occupied on other fronts these were days of economic prosperity and territorial expansion for Israel but God knew that, in His purposes, the Assyrians were to come down upon the ten tribes and lead them into a captivity from which they would never return. This was to happen in 721 B.C., probably within 50 years of Jonah receiving his commission to go to Nineveh, "that great city" established by Nimrod and notorious for its violence (Jonah 3:8). God was about to visit upon Israel a long captivity and in His all-seeing wisdom was preparing the way. Many and grievous would be the cries of a captive people for mercy to be shown by their captors "and it shall come to pass that, before they call, I will answer" (Isaiah 65:24). God was working His purposes out and Jonah was only one of the tools He was using and he probably never lived to see the reason for his mission.

It is clear that the prophet argued with God when the call first came. "Was not this my saying, when I was yet in my country" (Jonah 4:1,2). It was in his own country that Jonah first received the message for Nineveh and he apparently disputed the terms, saying in effect, "You are too merciful to destroy Nineveh with its vast population". But the persistency of the message continued and Jonah "rose up to flee unto Tarshish from the presence of the LORD". Whether this was the Tarshish in Spain or Tarsus in Cilicia (per Josephus) is irrelevant. It was a long way from Gath-hepher and from Israel.

Jeremiah eloquently tells of the effect on a prophet of an undeclared message: "And if I say, I will not make mention of Him, nor speak any more in His Name, then there is in mine heart as it were a burning fire shut up in my bones, and I am weary with forbearing, and I cannot contain" (Jeremiah 20:9). Amos puts it more picturesquely, "The lion hath roared, who will not fear? The Lord God hath spoken, who can but prophesy?" (Amos 3:8). Jonah should have been just as affected as those two prophets but "the fear of man bringeth a snare" (Proverbs 29:25) and the message was left unsaid. Jonah, with his deep knowledge of the Psalms (see the many quotations in chapter 2) would have known that it was impossible to get away from God (Psalm 139:9,10) but he hoped to avoid the all-pervading presence of God that he experienced in the land of Israel. Thus he went down to Joppa.

Physically there was no other way he could go when he left his native hills of Galilee for the sea-shore of Joppa; and spiritually, when a man leaves the presence of God there is no other way he can go but downwards. Mark the downward steps of the prophet "from the presence of the Lord ... down to Joppa ... found a ship ... going to Tarshish ... paid the fare ... went down into it ... to go with them ... down into the innermost parts of the ship ... and was fast asleep". At every stage of this downward path God was, as it were, giving him the opportunity to turn back to his mission. But no, Jonah "paid the fare" and was prepared to forfeit his life rather than forfeit his money. So deadened was he to that innermost voice that he fell into a trance-like sleep from which even the terrible storm could not awake him.

It is here that God launches the first of His special armoury of weapons, of which the sea-monster was only one, to effect His purposes through Jonah. A great wind, such as the hardy Phoenician sailors had never experienced, hit the ship bringing terror to all aboard. Jonah is dragged from his bed and his first sight of the storm and the terror of the seamen makes him realize that it was his cause that brought so much evil on his fellow men. The sailors cast the lots but though "the lot is cast into the lap ... the whole disposing thereof is of the LORD" (Proverbs 16:32). Jonah is now confronted by a handful of sailors who stare death in the face. God is giving him the opportunity of preaching to a few Gentiles to prepare him for the preaching to thousands in Nineveh.

Jonah takes up the challenge and testifies to those men of the greatness of his God would that we did the same more often when we too are face to face with our fellow men who tread that same road to dusty death. God in His turn honours His promise to all who call upon Him no matter who the preacher is. Jonah may not have been where God wanted him to be but the message is still blessed. Even so today, God blesses the work of all who serve Him, even if they have not seen the way to the house of God. Mark at this point Jonah's attitude to human life - he must be "thrown into the sea".

There is no question of a suicidal jump - Jonah knew he had no right to take his own life and that those men whose lives he had imperilled must take that irrevocable step. The result of the calming waters was to calm the minds of those sailors even as the calmed waters of Galilee stilled the anxious fears of the disciples. From then on, Jehovah was to be the God of these sailors and all false idols were to be dethroned. Maybe the captain put the ship back to Joppa for repairs and saw Jonah again after his ordeal in the fish. If so, the crew would have told him of the great calm that fell when Jonah was thrown overboard and would have heard in return of Jonah's miraculous preservation. God blessed that ship indeed and all who sailed in her.

The great fish prepared by God did its work. It provided a home for Jonah in which he could think out his position. There is no doubt that the days in the fish permanently marked Jonah as it has permanently marked other men who have had shorter experiences of the interior of sea monsters. Jonah's prayer in chapter 2 may be a summary of the many petitions that went up from this strangest of all prophets' chambers. The calming scriptures of the Psalms came time and again to his remembrance and are recorded imperishably in his prayer that ends with the realization to which myriads have been brought - "Salvation is of the Lord". Only the Lord who put him there can release him and this He did in His time and Jonah is vomited out upon dry land.

Jonah is now a man fully prepared for the Lord's work. He now goes to Nineveh without further argument, ready to preach against it. It would appear that the walls of Nineveh were circular and of such length that it would have taken three days to traverse them. Jonah may well have taken the west-east road across the diameter of the city which would thus have been a journey of one day. During that day, one can picture him stopping at each north-south intersection and giving Nineveh, forty days' notice of its destruction.

Many are the mentions of periods of forty in the Scriptures (Genesis 7:4; Exodus 24:18; Numbers 14:33,34; 1 Samuel 4:18; Matthew 4:2 and many others) and they invariably speak of a time of probation or testing. Thus it was with Nineveh, and the message from the marked man went home to the hearts of the people. We have already referred to the words of the Lord Jesus likening Jonah's time in the sea-monster to His time in the heart of the earth and Paul in Romans 6:3,4 speaking of baptism says, "all we who were baptized into Christ Jesus were baptized into His death. We were buried therefore with Him through baptism into death: that like as Christ was raised from the dead ..., so we also might walk in newness of life".

Baptized believers should, like Jonah, be marked men. If we were more so would not our testimony be as effective as Jonah's? As the common people of Nineveh looked on Jonah and heard his message repentance began with them and spread upwards through the nobles to the king who ordered a time of national repentance and mourning the effects of which spread even to the cattle, until all Nineveh is prostrate before the God with whom all have to deal.

It is in the last chapter that we see the anger and frustration of Jonah which caused C. H. Spurgeon, the great London preacher of the nineteenth century, to refer to him as "that unlovable prophet". But God loved him and, having prepared two special instruments to bring him to Nineveh, now prepares two more to move him to pity for the people. Jonah no doubt is angry at his own loss of face. He had foretold the destruction of Nineveh and that destruction had not come about. His very credibility as a prophet was at stake.

His prophecy to Jeroboam had been fulfilled but that to Nineveh had not and Jonah feels that God has let him down although at no time does he appear to have any anger or animos-

ity towards the people of Nineveh. His anger is directed sole-
ly against God who now shows him that divine love and pity
are not reserved exclusively for Israel but for all repentant crea-
tures. A gourd grows remarkably quickly to provide a shelter
for the prophet - possibly its growth hastened on by unexpect-
ed rains which may themselves have been harbingers of the relief of Nineveh.

How glad Jonah is of the shade the gourd gives from the hot
sun which, with his displeasure, has combined to put him in
an evil temper, but a worm, also prepared by God, destroys
the gourd as quickly as it grew. God then brings home to the
prophet the lesson He wanted to teach him. Jonah has done the
work he was sent to do and I suggest that Israel's coming generation were to rejoice that God had prepared the hearts of the
people of Nineveh to eschew violence and receive more gen-
tly than they otherwise would, a captive people. The ten tribes
were to be chastised through the captivity, but it was not God's
purpose that this chastisement should be tenfold worse at the
hands of an Assyrian people chafing at the destruction of their
chief city as foretold by a Hebrew prophet.

Return to Galilee, Jonah. Your work is done. Yes, out of Galilee
a prophet can arise (John 7:52) and in the fulness of time a
greater than Jonah will arise from those same Galilean hills
with a message not only for Israel but for the whole world.

CHAPTER TEN: MOSES (FRED EVANS)

―――

OF ALL THE DISTINGUISHED men of God, Moses stands out as one of the greatest. Different traits in his character and diverse aspects of his service come in for special mention in both the Old and New Testaments.

THE SERVANT

In the "great cloud of witnesses" in Hebrews 11, he is singled out for his faith in the true and living God. Having been cradled in his parents' faith at birth, he grew up with his own personal faith which enabled him to turn his eyes from the worldly considerations of life in the Egyptian palace and to fix them on the spiritual recompense. It was his faith that strengthened him to forsake Egypt, to limit his estimate of Pharaoh's power, and to highly esteem God's power and willingness to reward. It was faith in the word of God which gave him the power to institute and carry out the Passover, and also directed him to order the sprinkling of the blood on the doorposts:

> "By faith Moses, when he became of age, refused to be called the son of Pharaoh's daughter, choosing rather to suffer affliction with the people of God than to enjoy the passing pleasures of sin, esteeming the reproach of Christ greater riches than the treasures in Egypt; for he looked to the reward. By faith

he forsook Egypt, not fearing the wrath of the king; for he endured as seeing Him who is invisible. By faith he kept the Passover and the sprinkling of blood, lest he who destroyed the firstborn should touch them. By faith they passed through the Red Sea as by dry land, whereas the Egyptians, attempting to do so, were drowned" (Hebrews 11:23-28).

But it was not for faith alone that he was specially commended. It was also said of him, "The man Moses was very meek, above all the men which were upon the face of the earth". Wonderful praise indeed! Then again, in Jeremiah 15:1, he is singled out (with Samuel) as a man of outstanding interceding power, pleading with God for His people. Of him as a prophet the divine record states clearly that there had never been one like him in Israel, "whom the LORD knew face to face". No other prophet had equalled him in the great wonders and terrifying signs, in Egypt and in the sight of all Israel (Deuteronomy 34:10-12).

The title most frequently used of him in Scripture is "Moses the servant of the LORD", "Jehovah's servant". It seems to provide a cover for all his services and duties on God's behalf. When the Lord appointed Joshua to succeed Moses, He stated with loving and simple clarity, "Moses My servant is dead". It sounds almost as if it was an official title given to Moses, God having invested him with a special mission to make known His will. In so doing, He had conferred on him great honour and extensive authority.

THE PRINCE

Moses was born at a time of great depression in Israel's history. Various cruel attempts by the Egyptians to curb the population potential of the Hebrews had naturally disturbed the protective mother's mind, so that she devised means of keeping alive her attractive child. In the overruling providence of God, he was "drawn out of the water" of the Nile and adopted by one of Pharaoh's daughters.

The royal Princess reared Moses as her own son, and for almost forty years he lived in the environment of the royal court. Thus he was educated in all the wisdom and culture of the Egyptians and became powerful in speech and actions. Probably during this period his wise mother was in the position to fix in his mind the principles of devotion to the only true and living God. But this portion of his life ended abruptly when he defended and avenged one of his oppressed brethren by slaying the Egyptian.

Moses had gone out to visit his brethren and to witness with his own eyes their sufferings. In this way he made his open declaration of taking his part with the oppressed slaves on the grounds of their common kinship and inheritance of the promises of God. He clearly identified himself as "one of them". But he made the mistake of thinking that his own people would understand that God had chosen him to set them free, but they did not understand this.

Did the great Moses do wrong in killing the Egyptian? Under provocation, did he show a hasty impulsiveness or even resort to impetuous violence when he took the law into his own hands in killing the oppressor and hiding the body in the sand?

Whether the answer is yes or no, it is evident that the deliverance of the Israelites from Egypt did not take place for another 40 years. Pharaoh threatened his death, so Moses fled to the land of Midian.

THE REFUGEE

When Moses took refuge in Midian, he was content to dwell with Reuel and his family in a congenial home. In time he married Reuel's daughter, Zipporah, and they had two sons, Gershom and Eliezer. His wife probably died in the wilderness wanderings but little is known of his two sons. It is a tribute to his genuine and upright nature that they apparently took no prominent part in their tribe. He sought no self-seeking and practised no nepotism. Even at the close of his career, he followed implicitly the instructions of God, passing over his own family and choosing Joshua as his assistant and successor (Numbers 27:18, Joshua 1:1,2).

For forty years Moses experienced a background of solitude. What a change had taken place in his fortunes! Far from the stately home and his illustrious patroness! Away from his brethren and his people with whom he desired to be so closely identified! But his pastoral surroundings were conducive to his training in self-discipline, meekness and humble dependence on Jehovah. As a refugee shepherd sojourning in a foreign land he probably felt at times a sense of disappointment and even frustration. Yet God was preparing His man - trained in Egyptian skills and now being tempered in spirit in "the silent grandeur of the wilderness".

But the land of Midian contained Horeb, the mountain of God, Mount Sinai. Here the Lord appeared to him out of the bush which burned with fire but was not consumed (Exodus 3:1,2). This call set in motion a series of conversations in which the Lord graciously communed with His chosen servant, acquainting him of His purposes, revealing to him the part he would be expected to play in bringing His purposes to pass, and assuring him of the divine Presence throughout the programme. Jehovah called, equipped and commissioned Moses to be the instrument of deliverance, and gave him the superlative promise, "I will certainly be with you" (Exodus 3:12).

THE LEADER

The Lord, the God of the Hebrews was Jehovah, the great I AM. Moses was His servant appointed to deliver His people from Egypt, thus giving to God a "people for Himself". They were to be a Holy Nation, in covenant relationship with God, serving Him in His appointed way. In order that He might dwell among His people, it would be necessary for them to build for Him a sanctuary, a dwelling-place, according to the pattern which had been pre-arranged by God Himself. Moses was to be the human instrument for carrying out all this divine work. It was a tremendous task allotted to him, but to encourage him and to allay his fears and doubts the great God Himself promised forcibly to be present with him. Any diffidence or modesty on the part of Moses can be readily understood, for it was a gigantic task.

It is certainly necessary to point out that nothing but divine intervention enabled him to perform such exploits. His first efforts in Egypt only served to aggravate Pharaoh's sustained oppression and Israel's cruel bondage (Exodus 5:2-9). Moses was not eloquent and certainly not a rabble-raiser (Exodus 4:10). His solitary associate, humanly speaking, was his brother Aaron. Yet in a matter of months, without drawing a single Israelite sword, the departure of the Hebrews from Egypt was being urged by the Egyptians themselves. Their former oppressors gave them jewels of gold and silver, and clothing, thus enabling them to carry off the wealth of their taskmasters. Nothing but such plagues as God sent, and Scripture records, could have induced a dictatorial monarch like Pharaoh to allow such a humbling experience to overtake him.

In other ways God's miraculous powers were manifested. To lead an unwarlike nation of slaves out of a well-organized country like Egypt was a remarkable feat. The sustenance of 600,000 men besides women and children in a desert was a miracle made possible by the manna from heaven. To gain the acceptance by the Israelites, of the law which was so contrary to their corrupt inclinations and practices; to keep them together for forty years' wandering through the wearisome wilderness; and finally to lead them as far as the Jordan River - all these were remarkable achievements.

Throughout this period of faithful service, Moses manifested a spirit of meekness, patience, tenderness and long-suffering under great provocation and in numerous trials. His vigorous action and holy boldness for the Lord's honour were constantly accompanied by a devoted intercession for the people of God.

THE WRITER

Time and time again Moses was told by God to "write ... in a book" (e.g. Exodus 17:14, Numbers 33:2). And we are in the happy position of having examples of his prose and his poetry.

The "Five Books" of the Pentateuch really constitute one book divided into five sections, rather than five books merged into one. They are on scriptural authority ascribed to Moses. The main themes of the narrative relate to God's purposes in the world of fallen men, with special emphasis on the account of God's dealings with His chosen people. By no means is it a personal biography of the writer but like many other authors, Moses used throughout the well-known device of writing in the third person even when he himself was involved. In one strong characteristic Moses in the Pentateuch set the keynote to all succeeding prophets. Frequently he prefaced his remarks to the Israelites with the words, "The LORD spoke to Moses". This bears the true mark of the prophet of the Lord.

"Reckoning from Moses to Malachi we find a series of prophets who flourished in a continuous succession during a period of more than one thousand years; all confirming the authority of their predecessors; co-operating in the same designs; and uniting in one spirit to deliver the same doctrines, and to predict the same blessings to mankind" (Nicholson).

Happily, the writings of Moses were not confined to prose. Psalm 90 affords a suitable example, in the form of "A Prayer of Moses the Man of God". The humbling frailty of short-lived man is forcibly contrasted with the almighty power of the eternal God. Spurgeon suggested that the psalm provides a "specimen of the manner in which the seer of Horeb was wont to commune with heaven, and intercede for the good of Israel".

The song of triumph in Exodus 15 is among the oldest poems in the world, some even suggesting that it is the oldest by about 100 years. It abounds in incidents, marked by the freshness and simplicity to be expected from an eye-witness. In choice of event for commemoration, in selection of wording and phrasing, and in literary style, the song provides the ingredients for nobility and grandeur. The same may be said of the final song (Deuteronomy 33) and the blessing (chapter 34).

The songs of Moses laid a foundation for Israel's poetry and gave a tone to succeeding ages. In these circumstances, it comes as no surprise to learn from Revelation 15:2-4 that John, through the Holy Spirit, stated of the multitude of the victorious ones:

"They sing the song of Moses the servant of God, and the song of the Lamb, saying, Great and marvellous are Thy works, O Lord God, the Almighty; righteous and true are Thy ways, Thou King of the ages. Who shall not fear, O Lord, and glorify Thy name? For Thou only art holy".

CHAPTER ELEVEN: SAMUEL (JACK GAULT)

═══

HIS TIME

The days of Samuel were a watershed in the history of Israel. His work, under God, was to bring about the transition from the times of the Judges to the establishment of the kingdom under David. He came to Israel in a dark day when the nation was in a state of anarchy, the priesthood was corrupt and the Glory was about to depart from the house of God. Judges had come and gone, and each in his time and place had exerted his influence over the people, but after each one had died the people returned again to their old ways (Judges 2:18-19).

No man or tribe had been able to unite the people and bring them back to God. Israel needed such a man, and God had him ready. Samuel, the last of the Judges (Acts 13:20), would unite them and lead them again into the right paths.

HIS MOTHER

How strange and yet how wonderful are the ways of the Lord! To bring about His purposes for Israel, God dealt in a very special way with a woman of Ephraim. Sorrowing deeply because of her barrenness, but sensitive to the condition of her nation, she implored the Lord for a child. Her song of praise reveals an awareness of the sin of the people and shows her faith in her God. She was prepared to give her son to the service of the

Lord all his life. Out of the depths of her suffering she poured out her heart unto the Lord. From the Lord of Hosts (1 Samuel 1:11) she asked but for one, and the Lord heard and honoured her faith. She called her son's name Samuel, saying, "because I have asked him of the LORD".

The Lord frequently asks his servants to pass through the deep waters so that His purposes might be fulfilled and His name glorified. Hannah's sorrow was replaced by joy when she saw her son serving the Lord in His house. For the sake of the house of the Lord her God she was willing to sacrifice the company of her boy and to be content with an annual visit only. How selfless and faithful a woman she was and how worthwhile for her people was the sacrifice she made!

HIS CHILDHOOD

The story of the child Samuel belongs to our childhood. We loved to hear the story of the little boy in the Temple. He stands in so great a contrast to the aged Eli; so innocent among so much that was corrupt, so willing to serve and, when the voice of God came to him, so willing to listen. "Speak; for Your servant is listening". The boy, with his little robe and ephod was not, however, playing at priests in the house of God. He was ministering "unto the LORD before Eli". It was remarkable that Eli accepted his ministrations and one seems to gather that the old man was not unaware of the purposes of God regarding the lad. Perhaps his dealings with Hannah in the days of her sorrow and in the subsequent events, were the outcome of the old priest's perception under God of the events that lay ahead. Samuel, untouched by the sin and declension all around him, lived with the old man and was being prepared for his great work. "And Samuel grew, and the LORD was with him" (1 Samuel 3:19).

HIS CALL

As yet, Samuel had had no personal dealings with God. It was necessary that he must know God for himself and the day came when God spoke personally to him. Three times in the night the boy heard the voice of the Lord and three times thought that Eli had called to him. On the advice of the old man he waited for it once again, and for the fourth time the double call of his name was heard. This time Samuel said, "Speak; for Your servant is listening" and the Lord revealed to him the fearful events that were about to take place.

Like some of God's great men before and after him, Samuel received that repeated call which seems to signify that the one so called has a special place in the purposes of God with regard to His people.

Samuel became the custodian of those fateful prophecies concerning Israel, and after the death of Eli he became established, accepted by Israel as a prophet of the Lord (1 Samuel 3:20). The Lord spoke to Samuel and Samuel spoke to the people (1 Samuel 3:21 and 4:1).

Samuel would have witnessed the events of that disastrous day when the ark of the Lord was taken from Shiloh to the field of battle at Ebenezer. He would have seen the trembling of Eli and his anxiety for the safety of the ark. He would have been there when they heard the sad news from the man who returned from the battle, and would have seen the fatal results for Eli. Samuel must have been amazed when he heard also of the death of the two sons of Eli and the birth of Eli's grandson. The name, "Ichabod", did indeed describe the state of things for Israel; could they sink any lower?

HIS WORK

For the next twenty years or so Samuel lived at Ramah. The Tabernacle was forsaken; the ark was in custody at Kiriath-jearim; there was no sacrifice or offering and no priest functioned before the Lord. Samuel kept in close touch with God. He called his sons Joel (Jehovah is God) and Abijah (Jehovah is Father) telling us that Samuel stayed close to the Lord throughout those dark days. He was a man of prayer (1 Samuel 7:5, 8:6) and of blameless life. He itinerated around the land, judging the people, teaching and exhorting them to return to the Lord.

At an appropriate moment he summoned all Israel to Mizpah. He called upon them to put away their idols and to serve Jehovah only. His long struggle was successful for they put away their Baalim and Ashtaroth and were united in their rededication of themselves to the Lord. Encouraged by their new condition they routed the Philistines, and Samuel raised a Stone of Remembrance as a token of the Lord's help.

Samuel's supremacy in Israel was now established beyond question and the Philistines returned no more in his day. A new spirit was abroad in the nation.

HIS DISAPPOINTMENT

When the people asked for a king, Samuel was displeased and disappointed; not only for his own sake, but also for the Lord's. Characteristically he took the matter to the Lord, and the Lord heard. "They have not rejected thee, but they have rejected Me", the Lord said to Samuel. He shared Samuel's disappointment, but it was only another incident in the long history of such disappointments and griefs that God had endured from His people. Nor would it end here. For centuries to come He was to know their backsliding and disobedience which would reach a climax in the rejection of their Messiah.

From the people's point of view they could see no successor to Samuel. He was now old, his sons were failures and not likely to succeed their father. There was no one else of his stature to look to and they saw the other nations with their kings. The elders of Israel were obviously concerned, and made request to Samuel for a king. Perhaps they feared a return to the old ways and a return of their old enemies to trouble them. Once again the Lord had His man ready. He had revealed His purposes to Samuel, and the man who was every inch a king was anointed as ruler of Israel. It is typical of Samuel that although he disliked what had taken place, he accepted the will of God and became closely involved with the new king. By Samuel's help and encouragement Saul was established in Israel and Samuel wrote the nation's new constitution in a book and laid it up before the Lord (1 Samuel 10:25).

All might have been well, but in divine foreknowledge, the sceptre belonged to Judah (Genesis 49:10) and the boy of the family of Jesse who was keeping his father's sheep on the hills of Judea was destined to be the founder of Israel's dynasty of whom would be the Christ of Israel, God blessed for evermore. It was typical again of the man Samuel and his largeness of heart that when Saul sinned and was rejected by the Lord, Samuel mourned for him (1 Samuel 15:35).

HIS CHALLENGE

Samuel was old, and must go the way of all the earth. He had lived through momentous days in Israel's history. He had controlled, under God, the destiny of His people. He had rescued them from anarchy and idolatry and had made them again function as a nation, establishing them again before the Lord. He was unique in that from childhood, throughout all his life, he had exerted an influence for good over the nation of Israel, and had been at the centre of their affairs.

His life was one of integrity and righteousness. His character was unblemished; no mistakes, no moral lapses, no disobedience, no selfishness, is recorded. Honest with God and with His people. Wise and impartial in his judgements, he is in some respects unequalled in all Israel's history.

On one remarkable day, with courage and confidence, he publicly challenged Israel to declare if they had any word to say against him. "And they said, You have not cheated us or oppressed us, nor have you taken anything from any man's hand". And Samuel said unto them, "The LORD is witness against you, and His anointed is witness this day, that ye have not found anything in my hand". And they said, "He is witness" (1 Samuel 12:1-5). It is given to few men to attain such a standing and reputation among their fellows.

HIS OLD AGE AND DEATH

The old and grey-headed Samuel (1 Samuel 12:2) was not permitted to have an undisturbed retirement. As always, in times of crisis, they came to Samuel for counsel (1 Samuel 19:18). The last days of Saul's rule were troubled days for Israel. The demented king, forsaken by God, turned to witchcraft for guidance and comfort. Even in death the old man was not allowed to sleep undisturbed but rather returned under God to announce the new kingdom. How remarkable the man was and such his standing in Israel that even after death he was called upon to make known the mind of the Lord concerning the kingdom!

CHAPTER TWELVE: JOHN THE BAPTIST (JOHN TERRELL)

———

"WHAT WENT YE OUT INTO the wilderness to behold?", the Lord demanded of those around Him - people who may have overheard the appeal for re-assurance which John made from his dismal cell in the fortress of Machaerus. Let none of them be in doubt for a moment about the spiritual and moral stature of this rugged and fearless character. We do not readily appreciate the far-reaching nature of Christ's assessment, "Among them that are born of women there hath not arisen a greater than John the Baptist" (Matthew 11:11); nor His following pronouncement, "Yet he that is but little in the kingdom of heaven is greater than he". Herein lies the secret of the vast superiority of the New Covenant whose divine Messenger was foretold by Malachi, the same prophet as spoke of "My messenger ... (who) shall prepare the way before Me" (Malachi 3:1). The former was the Lord from heaven Himself, the latter His noble cousin and forerunner, John.

It was given, appropriately, to Luke the beloved physician to record the intimate narrative of the births of both Jesus and John. For Luke presents these sacred events very much as an integrated sequence in which the advent of the Lord and the appearance of the Baptist are evidently inseparable in the divine purpose of grace. This is but one of the indications in the New Testament of the unique distinction of the last of the worthy men of God who, in the Old Covenant context, were called "the prophets". None was more acutely conscious than John of the surpassing excellence of the One "the latchet of whose shoe I am not worthy to unloose"; yet in the same narrative which contains the angelic prediction of Christ, "He shall be great, and shall be called the Son of the Most High", the Holy Spirit records of John that, "he shall be great in the sight of the Lord" (Luke 1:32,15). Furthermore, Zacharias, filled with the Holy Spirit, exclaims joyfully, "Thou, child, shalt be called the prophet of the Most High" (Luke 1:76).

We would wish to stay with the story of John's birth, if space allowed, to enter into the holy joy of the godly Elisabeth as she joins the blessed company of good women of Scripture who realized the promise of a son, beyond all natural laws or human expectation - Sarah, Hannah, and the wife of Manoah. As we listen to the wondering of the Judeans about John, "What then shall this child be?" (Luke 1:66) we cannot but recall the devout question of Manoah, Samson's father, "What shall be the manner of the child, and what shall be his work?" (Judges 13:12). We have seen that the Spirit left Zacharias in no doubt about the glory of John's ministry and to this prospect Zacharias gave voice in the choice psalm of Luke 1:67-79, words which richly repay prayerful meditation, and which close on the sweetest of notes, "Whereby the Dayspring from on high shall visit us, to shine upon them that sit in darkness and the shadow of death; to guide our feet into the way of peace".

And so into the obscurity of the wilderness preparation years went the chosen young Nazirite, while up in Nazareth his carpenter Cousin learned the skills of the bench and "opened His ear morning by morning". Speculation about John's possible early association with the Essene sect, of Dead Sea Scrolls fame, is of little relevance to Scripture revelation. For John's insight into his mission was clear; indeed acutely so, as the Gospel according to John makes plain. 'There came a man, sent from God, and, "He that sent me ... said unto me, Upon whomsoever thou shalt see the Spirit descending ... the same is He ..." (John 1:6,33); and Luke declares that "the word of God came unto John ... in the wilderness" (Luke 3:2). The voice of God was unmistakable to the man whose own distinctive title was to be "the voice of one crying in the wilderness".

Thus he described himself to the enquiring priests and Levites, the emissaries of the Jerusalem Pharisees who evidently recognized a man of commanding religious significance in their midst (John 1:19-28). The time of John's revealing to Israel had come and the nation's leaders were quite unprepared for either the messenger or his message. Rugged, fearless and faithful as Elijah, in whose spirit and power he came, John entertained no compromise with hypocritical Pharisees and Sadducees who came to his baptism - a baptism which was indeed "unto the remission of sins" but in which a false profession was both ineffectual and anathema to the baptizer. "Ye offspring of vipers...".

These have their counterpart today in lip-servers of a form of godliness but who have denied the power. Repentance, evidenced by its fruits, was his unsparing demand, with inevitable judgement as the only alternative. The path prepared for the coming divine baptizer in the Holy Spirit must be undeviatingly straight. Wholly expendable in his dedication to his mission, John ploughed a furrow that was totally true. What a joy and strength it must have been to the Lord as His footsteps approached Jordan's banks, to observe His forerunner's complete integrity.

Now the cry so long awaited by a sin-weary creation rings out, "Behold, the Lamb of God, which taketh away the sin of the world!" a witness little understood or appreciated, no doubt, by the multitude, but one which appealed to the hearts of men whom God was preparing for His Son's service. So we read that "the two disciples heard him speak, and they followed Jesus" - precious words to be cherished by any witness to the saving Name of Christ and His call to discipleship. Perhaps John, son of Zebedee, the writer of these words (John 1:37) was one of the two; certainly Andrew was one and his immediate and spontaneous concern for his brother Simon glows heart-warmingly from the sacred page. John must have rejoiced, but with a little pang, as he generously relinquished his best men to a service infinitely higher and nobler.

Resolute in his rebuke alike of serf and monarch, John soon looks out from Herod's prison bars. It was this worthless king's crowning act of pique and cowardice that he "added yet this above all, that he shut up John in prison". Yet, in the sovereign purpose of God and of His Christ, this was apparently the moment for the Lord to enter into His main Galilean ministry (Matthew 4:12; Mark 1:14). The people that sat in darkness were about to experience a great light. Although John was careful to describe himself only as coming "to bear witness of the Light" (John 1:7) the Lord offers generous praise of His herald, "He was the lamp that burneth and shineth: and ye were willing to rejoice for a season in his light" (John 5:35).

Meanwhile the Lord graciously awaits the transfer of allegiance of some of John's disciples whose loyalty to their early master is touching in its constancy. Both Mark (2:18) and Luke (5:33-39) recount the question to Jesus concerning fasting, and the patient but radical teaching of the Master about the presence of the Bridegroom, and the new wine for fresh wineskins. Indeed, one of John's most telling descriptions is "the friend of the Bridegroom", borrowing its message of intimacy from the Jewish marriage ceremony with its rich pageantry.

And so the iron enters into the soul of the weary prisoner in his lonely dungeon. Again these dear devoted men convey their leader's message to Jesus, "Art Thou He that cometh, or look we for another?" Back comes the re-assuring evidence of the outflowing blessings of the proclaimed kingdom. And for those around who listened the Lord issued His glowing tribute to "a prophet ... and much more than a prophet". We almost feel sad that the messengers of John had departed and were not able to report to him the warm eulogy which the Lord Jesus made to the multitude.

But the beloved Baptist had few more days left in which to languish in Herod's pit of suffering. The cell door swung open and in moments the great man's service and suffering were at an end. No nobler head, alive or dead, ever graced a royal banquet. But for that deed of squalid cowardice the divine assize will exact an appropriate penalty. When devoted disciple hands had buried John and the news reached Jesus, He withdrew seeking the quietness for which the grieving spirit longs.

The law and the prophets, we are instructed, were until John (Luke 16:16). We are conscious of standing at a unique milestone in divine purposes as the last representative of the dispensation of law embraces, on the banks of the Jordan, the One 'full of grace and truth'. God's purpose, in the ultimate, is one, and each development is articulated beautifully to the next. We stand today, it may well be, on the threshold of God's next major initiative - the personal return of His beloved Son. Perhaps John's camel-hair coat and leather girdle have a message for our hearts, which are so readily seduced by the myriad appeals of the world around. Should our pre-occupation be in any way different from the heroic Baptist's? "Behold, the Lamb of God".

CHAPTER THIRTEEN: NATHAN (GEORGE PRASHER SNR.)

———

MESSAGES FROM MANY prophets appear in the historical parts of the Holy Scriptures. To some of these we wish to draw attention. Firstly we note that Miriam and Deborah are spoken of as prophetesses at times of great deliverances from Israel's enemies. Then we have two unnamed prophets who spoke from God, one to Israel early in the dark days of the Judges (Judges 6:8); and one to Eli the priest because of his failure to control his sons.

Later through Nathan came very important tidings to David. The king, musing on God's goodness to him, decided to build a house for God, because the divine dwelling was one of curtains only. The proposal was pleasing to the prophet, but the LORD made it known that David was not to have this honour, because he was a man of blood. It was reserved for his son who would sit upon his throne. So "Solomon built Him a house" (Acts 7:47). From this we learn it is no small matter to be permitted to build a house for the LORD. This is true whether we think of days of triumph and glory, as were the days of Solomon; or remnant days, as were the days of Zerubbabel. Would that this were better appreciated in our own day and time! When the Remnant started to build the house in the days of Haggai the prophet, the LORD repeated the encouraging words, "I am with you", and added, "I will bless you". Then beautiful is the promise, "In this place will I give peace" (Haggai 1:2).

Nathan had yet another communication for David. At the return of the year, at the time when kings go out to battle, David sent Joab and his servants to destroy the children of Ammon, but he himself stayed at Jerusalem. He was reclining at ease while his servants were bearing the brunt of the battle. It was then he saw and took Bathsheba, the wife of Uriah. In addition he planned and brought about the death of that valiant soldier. Concerning all this we read, "But the thing that David had done displeased the LORD" (2 Samuel 11).

By the time that Nathan was sent to David the child by Bathsheba was born. Fully nine months had passed since that fateful day when he sinned against God. During these many months he had covered up his sin. Unconfessed sin brings a cloud between God and His servant. They were months of silence and roaring -silence in respect to his guilt, and roaring because of his misery. Fellowship with God was lost, the heavens became brass and the earth iron, peace and comfort were not to be found. Psalm 32 reveals much in David's experience. He says, "When I kept silence, my bones waxed old, through my roaring all the day long. For day and night Thy hand was heavy upon me: My moisture was changed as with the drought of summer. (Selah)." True are the words of Isaiah 59:2, "Your iniquities have separated between you and your God, and your sins have hid His face from you, that He will not hear".

At length God intervenes and Nathan is sent with his message. It concerned a poor man who owned a ewe lamb that he had brought up and was like a daughter to him, and a rich man who possessed flocks and herds, but when a visitor came he spared to take of his own flock, but took the poor man's lamb and dressed it for the man that was come to him. As David listened his anger was greatly kindled. He judged the man to be worthy of death, and he commanded that he restore the lamb fourfold. To this Nathan replied, "Thou art the man". In this manner David's sin was brought home to him, and he said, "I have sinned against the LORD".

Nathan was faithful to inform David that judgement from the LORD would come upon him. It is ever true that "God is not mocked: for whatsoever a man soweth, that shall he also reap. For he that soweth unto his own flesh shall of the flesh reap corruption; but he that soweth unto the Spirit shall of the Spirit reap eternal life" (Galatians 6:7,8). "Now therefore", said the LORD, "the sword shall never depart from thine house", and, "I will raise up evil against thee out of thine own house ... For thou didst it secretly: but I will do this thing before all Israel, and before the sun." David by his actions had despised his God, and besides the above judgements that would come upon him, the child would surely die.

When David had confessed his sin, immediately God said through Nathan, "The LORD also hath put away thy sin; thou shalt not die." Wonderful must have been the joy and comfort that these words brought to David. He had pronounced the death sentence upon himself, but the LORD forgave the now contrite sinner. No longer is his moisture changed as with the drought of summer, for he says, "I acknowledged my sin unto Thee, and mine iniquity have I not hid: I said, I will confess my

transgressions unto the LORD; and Thou forgavest the iniquity of my sin" (Psalm 32:5). In the joy of sins forgiven he sings:
"Blessed is he whose transgression is forgiven, whose sin is covered. Blessed is the man unto whom the LORD imputeth not
iniquity, and in whose spirit there is no guile."

He had cast himself upon the mercy of God, and Psalm 51
shows that his sorrow and repentance were deep and real: "A
broken and a contrite heart, O God, Thou wilt not despise".
With the writer of Psalm 119:145 he could say, "I have called
with my whole heart; answer me, O LORD". The mercy and
the judgement revealed in this story recall the words of Psalm
99 verse 8, "Thou answeredst them, O LORD our God: Thou
wast a God that forgavest them, Though Thou tookest
vengeance of their doings."

And of the word spoken through angels we are told, "Every
transgression and disobedience received a just recompense of
reward," and the solemn question presents itself to us, "How
shall we escape, if we neglect so great salvation?" (Hebrews
2:2,3).

CHAPTER FOURTEEN: GAD (GEORGE PRASHER SNR.)

———

GAD IS ANOTHER PROPHET through whom God spoke to David. His first message recorded in 1 Samuel 22:5 is brief. David was enduring severe trials through the persecutions of Saul. He had got away from the court of Achish, the king of the Philistines, where he had feigned madness, and escaped to the cave of Adullam. "When his brethren and all his father's house heard it, they went down thither to him. And every one that was in distress, and every one that was in debt, and every one that was discontented, gathered themselves unto him; and he became captain over them: and there were with him about four hundred men." These recognized in David the one whom the Lord had anointed. They took their place under him.

It is good when exercised ones, having become discontented and distressed because of the self-will of men in sectarianism, gather themselves to our David, the Lord Jesus Christ, in this day of His rejection. He is the "Living Stone, rejected indeed of men, but with God elect, precious." Such as go forth to Him may be "built up a spiritual house, to be a holy priesthood, to offer up spiritual sacrifices, acceptable to God through Jesus Christ" (1 Peter 2:4,5).

Gad's message was, "Abide not in the hold; depart, and get thee into the land of Judah." So "David departed, and came into the forest of Hereth" (1 Samuel 22:5). In this manner the LORD gave guidance to David, and it is pleasing to note David's response to the word of God. It was of great comfort to God's servant to receive instruction from heaven as to his movements in a time of peril. The prolonged tyranny of Saul was allowed as a test for the man destined to hold the most responsible position in Israel. However, it is true what has been said, "If God proved men by their trials, they proved God in their trials." The Book of the Psalms reveals this truth. In his psalms David reveals his trust in the God whom he had proved to be his lovingkindness, his fortress, his high tower, his deliverer, and his shield (Psalm 144:2). Let us remember that the proof of our faith is more precious than gold that perishes though it is proved by fire.

Another word reached David through the prophet Gad. The circumstances are recorded in 2 Samuel 24, and 1 Chronicles 21. "The anger of the LORD was kindled against Israel, and He moved David against them, saying, Go, number Israel and Judah." In the Chronicles we read, "And Satan stood up against Israel, and moved David to number Israel." It is evident there was sin among God's people that had aroused His anger, and judgement must be brought upon them. In this instance it comes about through God allowing Satan to work through David. David said to Joab, "Go now ... number ye the people, that I may know the sum of the people." "The king's word was abominable to Joab." Was David compelled to follow Satan's movings in this matter? We believe not. Satan moved against the Son of God in the wilderness, tempting Him, but He countered each movement of the adversary by a saying of God. But David failed. If the business was abominable to Joab, why was it desirable to David? Was he caught up in an unguarded hour? It may be so. However, the lesson for us is plain:

Yield not to temptation,

For yielding is sin,

Each victory will help you

Some other to win.

Fight manfully onward,

Dark passions subdue,

Look ever to Jesus,

He'll carry you through.

The king at length awoke to realize his sin, and he confessed his foolishness to God. It was then that Gad was commissioned to say to David:

> "Thus saith the LORD, I offer thee three things; choose thee one of them, that I may do it unto thee ... Take which thou wilt; either three years of famine; or three months to be consumed before thy foes, while that the sword of thine enemies overtaketh thee; or else three days the sword of the LORD destroying throughout all the coasts of Israel ... And David said unto Gad, I am in a great strait: let me fall now into the hand of the LORD; for very great are His mercies: and let me not fall into the hand of man."

Seventy thousand men of Israel fell, and the angel of the LORD was about to destroy Jerusalem when the LORD said, "It is enough; now stay thine hand." This was at the threshing-floor of Ornan the Jebusite. Gad was commanded to tell David to rear an altar unto the LORD on this threshing-floor. This David did, and the LORD answered him from heaven by fire upon the altar of burnt offering. When David saw that God so answered him at the threshing-floor, he sacrificed there, and said, "This is the house of the LORD God, and this is the altar of burnt offering for Israel."

Let us note that David had a true sense of values. Ornan was generous to offer the oxen for burnt offering, the threshing instruments for wood, and the wheat for the meal offering, but David would not offer a burnt offering without cost. "I will verily buy it for the full price," said David. It was here Solomon built "the house of the LORD at Jerusalem in mount Moriah, where the Lord appeared unto David his father, which he made ready in the place that David had appointed, in the threshing-floor of Ornan the Jebusite" (2 Chronicles 3:1). Wonderful indeed were the blessings that accrued from scenes of the LORD's judgements! We also can say, "With mercy and with judgement my web of time He wove."

CHAPTER FIFTEEN: AHIJAH THE SHILONITE (GEORGE PRASHER SNR.)

NOW WE WISH TO GIVE thought to some words from Ahijah, the Shilonite. Two men were in a field alone, one the prophet Ahijab, the other Jeroboam, the son of Nebat. Jeroboam was an active person whose industry and valour attracted the attention of the king, and Solomon promoted him to have charge of all the labour of the house of Joseph. It was then, as it is now, "A man's gift maketh room for him, and bringeth him before great men" (Proverbs 18:16). Well, when Ahijah met this young man in the field he was clad in a new garment which he tore in twelve pieces, ten of which he gave to Jeroboam, saying, "Take thee ten pieces: for thus saith the Lord, the God of Israel, Behold, I will rend the kingdom out of the hand of Solomon, and will give ten tribes to thee: (but he shall have one tribe, for My servant David's sake, and for Jerusalem's sake, the city which I have chosen)" (1 Kings 11:28-32).

The LORD loved Solomon from his birth, and even before his birth had determined that he should reign as king. Although he had older brothers, and one at least was the son of a princess, yet when the time arrived Solomon sat upon the throne of David his father. The LORD made him to prosper above all that were before him, or that followed after, for "God gave Solomon wisdom and understanding exceeding much, and largeness of heart, even as the sand that is on the sea shore" (1

Kings 4:29). God was faithful in all His promises. Why this dreadful change in the Lord's attitude to Solomon? What has occurred that the kingdom must be torn from him, or from his son? The story is a sad one, for though the LORD had been faithful, Solomon had failed to obey the commands of his God. Even he found that a full cup was not easily carried. His tenure of favour with the LORD was conditioned by obedience to the LORD.

According to the law of the LORD, the king must not multiply wives to himself, that his heart turn not away; nor was he to multiply horses to himself, nor cause the people to return to Egypt; neither was he to multiply to himself silver and gold. Yet instead of subjecting himself to the will of God, we read, "Now king Solomon loved many strange women, together with the daughter of Pharaoh, women of the Moabites, Ammonites, Edomites, Zidonians, and Hittites; of the nations concerning which the LORD said unto the children of Israel, Ye shall not go among them neither shall they come among you: for surely they will turn away your heart after their gods: Solomon clave unto these in love" (1 Kings 11:1,2). He also multiplied his horses, his silver and gold. "When Solomon was old," we are told, "his wives turned away his heart after their gods." He even built a high place for Chemosh, the abomination of Moab, in the mount that is before Jerusalem, and for Molech, the abomination of the children of Ammon. And he did so for all his strange wives, who burned incense and sacrificed unto their gods. Long years later, Nehemiah commented on Solomon's actions in these words: "Even him did strange women cause to sin" (Nehemiah 13:26).

The LORD was angry with Solomon, because his heart was turned away from the LORD ... who had appeared unto him twice, and had commanded him concerning this thing. "Forasmuch as this is done of thee," said the LORD, "and thou hast not kept My covenant and My statutes, which I have commanded thee, I will surely rend the kingdom from thee, and will give it to thy servant."

In His patience, the LORD waited till the death of Solomon before he brought the judgement. Rehoboam, his son, came to the throne. Jeroboam, learning that Solomon was dead, returned from Egypt, whither he had fled from the wrath of Solomon, and he with all the congregation came to Rehoboam with a grievance. They wished the yoke of Solomon made lighter. Taking the advice of the younger men, which was really foolish advice, the king gave answer that he would make the yoke heavier, and he would chastise them with scorpions. The response of the people was, "What portion have we in David? ... to your tents, O Israel." Thus the ten tribes revolted, and Rehoboam was left with a small remnant of the nation. There were now two kingdoms, and betimes wars broke out, with their accompanying sorrows and loss. Let us note, in passing, that the results of sin are far-reaching. The folly to which the wisest of men stooped bore grievous fruit during many years that followed. It was the folly of disobeying the clear commands of the LORD.

Let us now think of Ahijah's message to Jeroboam. He was to reign over the ten tribes, and God said, "It shall be, if thou wilt hearken unto all that I command thee, and wilt walk in My ways, and do that which is right in Mine eyes, to keep My statutes and My commandments, as David My servant did; that I will be with thee, and will build thee a house, as I built for David, and will give Israel unto thee" (1 Kings 11:37,38).

Here was a grand opportunity for this young man. How would he react! Jerusalem was the place where God ordained that men should worship, because His house was there, and He had placed His Name there. But Jeroboam considered, "If this people go up to offer sacrifices in the house of the LORD at Jerusalem, then shall the heart of this people turn again unto their lord, even unto Rehoboam king of Judah; and they shall kill me" (1 Kings 12:27). So he took counsel, and made two calves of gold, placing one in Beth-el and one in Dan, and said to his people, "It is too much for you to go up to Jerusalem; Behold thy gods, O Israel, which brought thee up out of the land of Egypt ... And this thing became a sin: for the people went to worship before each of them, even unto Dan" (1 Kings 12:28,30, RV margin).

Resorting to human reasoning, he acted thus, arranging a spurious worship, with priests not of the sons of Levi, and feasts in imitation of the feasts of the LORD. The promised blessing that Ahijah mentioned could not be his, but stern and awful judgement made known to him through the same prophet Ahijah. Every man child of his would be cut off, and his house utterly swept away, as a man sweepeth away dung, till all be gone. Jeroboam is known as the man who made Israel to sin. When Baasha came to the throne, "he smote all the house of Jeroboam; he left not to Jeroboam any that breathed, until he had destroyed him; according to the saying of the LORD, which He spake by the hand of His servant Ahijah the Shilonite" (1 Kings 14 and 15).

We close our remarks on the prophecy through Ahijah with the words of Proverbs 8.34-36:

> "Blessed is the man that heareth me, watching daily at my gates, waiting at the posts of my doors. For whoso findeth me findeth life, and shall obtain favour of the LORD. But he that sinneth against me wrongeth his own soul: all they that hate me love death."

Did you love *Profiles of the Prophets*? Then you should read *Back to Basics: A Guide to Essential Bible Teaching* by Hayes Press!

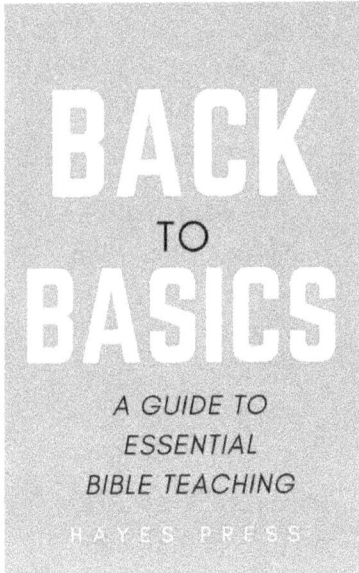

This book uses a combination of teaching and practical content and study questions to explore 8 key topics that are essential to the Christian faith: Knowing God, Salvation, Believer's Baptism, The Breaking of Bread, Understanding The Bible, The Return of Jesus Christ, Spiritual Gifts, Church Life - Why, what, where? This book contains a section of study questions and is ideal for personal or group Bible study.

Also by Hayes Press

The Road Through Calvary: 40 Devotional Readings
Lovers of God's House
Different Discipleship: Jesus' Sermon on the Mount
The House of God: Past, Present and Future
The Kingdom of God
Knowing God: His Names and Nature
Churches of God: Their Biblical Constitution and Functions
Four Books About Jesus
Collected Writings On ... Exploring Biblical Fellowship
Collected Writings On ... Exploring Biblical Hope
Collected Writings On ... The Cross of Christ
Builders for God
Collected Writings On ... Exploring Biblical Faithfulness
Collected Writings On ... Exploring Biblical Joy
Possessing the Land: Spiritual Lessons from Joshua
Collected Writings On ... Exploring Biblical Holiness
Collected Writings On ... Exploring Biblical Faith
Collected Writings On ... Exploring Biblical Love
These Three Remain...Exploring Biblical Faith, Hope and
Love
The Teaching and Testimony of the Apostles
Pressure Points - Biblical Advice for 20 of Life's Biggest Challenges
More Than a Saviour: Exploring the Person and Work of Jesus
The Psalms: Volumes 1-4 Boxset
The Faith: Outlines of Scripture Doctrine
Key Doctrines of the Christian Gospel
Is There a Purpose to Life?
Bible Covenants 101
The Hidden Christ - Volume 2: Types and Shadows in Offerings and Sacrifices

The Hidden Christ Volume 1: Types and Shadows in the Old Testament
The Hidden Christ - Volume 3: Types and Shadows in Genesis
Heavenly Meanings - The Parables of Jesus
Fisherman to Follower: The Life and Teaching of Simon Peter
Called to Serve: Lessons from the Levites
Needed Truth 2017 Issue 1
The Breaking of the Bread: Its History, Its Observance, Its Meaning
Spiritual Revivals of the Bible
An Introduction to the Book of Hebrews
The Holy Spirit and the Believer
The Psalms: Volume 1 - Thoughts on Key Themes
The Psalms: Volume 2 - Exploring Key Elements
The Psalms: Volume 3 - Surveying Key Sections
The Psalms: Volume 4 - Savouring Choice Selections
Profiles of the Prophets
The Hidden Christ - Volumes 1-4 Box Set
The Hidden Christ - Volume 4: Types and Shadows in Israel's Tabernacle
Baptism - Its Meaning and Teaching
Conflict and Controversy in the Church of God in Corinth
In the Shadow of Calvary: A Bible Study of John 12-17
Moses: God's Deliverer
Sparkling Facets: The Names and Titles of Jesus
A Little Book About Being Christlike
Keys to Church Growth
From Shepherd Boy to Sovereign: The Life of David
Back to Basics: A Guide to Essential Bible Teaching
An Introduction to the Holy Spirit
Israel and the Church in Bible Prophecy

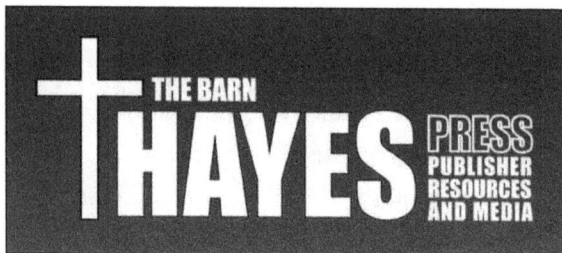

About the Publisher

Hayes Press (www.hayespress.org) is a registered charity in the United Kingdom, whose primary mission is to disseminate the Word of God, mainly through literature. It is one of the largest distributors of gospel tracts and leaflets in the United Kingdom, with over 100 titles and hundreds of thousands despatched annually. In addition to paperbacks and eBooks, Hayes Press also publishes Plus Eagles Wings, a fun and educational Bible magazine for children, and Golden Bells, a popular daily Bible reading calendar in wall or desk formats. Also available are over 100 Bibles in many different versions, shapes and sizes, Bible text posters and much more!

www.ingramcontent.com/pod-product-compliance
Lightning Source LLC
Chambersburg PA
CBHW021203020426
42331CB00003B/183